People, Places, and Things 3

Reading · Vocabulary · Test Preparation

Lin Lougheed

OXFORD
UNIVERSITY PRESS

OXFORD
UNIVERSITY PRESS

198 Madison Avenue
New York, NY 10016 USA

Great Clarendon Street, Oxford OX2 6DP UK

Oxford University Press is a department of the University of Oxford.
It furthers the University's objective of excellence in research, scholarship,
and education by publishing worldwide in

Oxford New York

Auckland Cape Town Dar es Salaam Hong Kong Karachi
Kuala Lumpur Madrid Melbourne Mexico City Nairobi
New Delhi Shanghai Taipei Toronto

With offices in

Argentina Austria Brazil Chile Czech Republic France Greece
Guatemala Hungary Italy Japan Poland Portugal Singapore
South Korea Switzerland Thailand Turkey Ukraine Vietnam

OXFORD and OXFORD ENGLISH are registered trademarks of
Oxford University Press

© Oxford University Press 2006

Database right Oxford University Press (maker)

Library of Congress Cataloging-in-Publication Data
Lougheed, Lin, 1946–
    People, places, and things : reading, vocabulary, test preparation / Lin Lougheed.
        p. cm.
    Includes indexes.
    ISBN-13: 978-0-19-430202-9 (student bk. : level 3)
    ISBN-10: 0-19-430202-4 (student bk. : level 3)
[etc.]
    1. English language—Textbooks for foreign speakers. English language—
Examinations—Study guides. I. Title.
    PE1128.L648 2005
    428'.0076—dc22

                                              2005049800

Executive Publisher: Nancy Leonhardt
Senior Acquisitions Editor: Chris Balderston
Editor: Anna Teevan
Assistant Editor: Kate Schubert
Art Director: Maj-Britt Hagsted
Senior Designer: Mia Gomez
Art Editor: Robin Fadool
Production Manager: Shanta Persaud
Production Controller: Zai Jawat Ali

Additional realia by Mia Gomez

ISBN-13: 978 0 19 430202 9
ISBN-10: 0 19 430202 4

10 9 8 7 6 5 4 3 2 1

Printed in Hong Kong.

Acknowledgments:

Cover photographs: Lee Young-Pyo: AP Photo/Hussein Malla; Mount Lhotse and
Mount Everest: ©Brad Wrobleski/Masterfile; Stonehenge: ©SuperStock/Alamy;
Chinese Dragon: ©ImageState/Alamy; Tropical fish: ©ImageState/Alamy;
Midori Ito: ©Neal Preston/CORBIS.

We would like to thank the following for their permission to reproduce
photographs:

Corbis: Warren Morgan p.2; Robertstock.com p.4; Korean American Students at
Yale, KASY p.6; Peter Arnold, Inc.: Sylvain Cordier p.12; Seapics.com p.14;
Seapics.com p.16; Associated Press, AP: Domenico Stinellis p.22; Reuters/Corbis:
Michael Dalder p.24; Associated Press, AP: Dusan Vranic p.26; Globe Photos:
Gareth Gay - Alpha Photo Press Agency Ltd. p.32; Leonardo Mattioli p.34;
Workbook Stock.com p.36; The Image Finders p.42; Danita Delmont: David Wall
Photography p.44; Robert Harding Picture Library Ltd/Alamy p.46; Corbis: W.
Perry Conway p.52; Image Quest p.54; Ardea p.56; Bettmann/Corbis p.62; Joe
Viesti Photography p.64; Stone/Getty: Julie Troy p.66; Associated Press, AP:
Andy Wong p.72; Corbis: Roger Ressmeyer p.74; Associated Press, AP p.76.

CONTENTS

TO THE TEACHER

Welcome to *People, Places, and Things*.

What is in each unit?

Prepare to Read

This section introduces the topic of the passage. The questions encourage students to share their own thoughts and experiences, and they can be used for discussion before reading.

Word Focus

This matching activity introduces students to new or unfamiliar words that they will see in the reading passage. Students match the ten words with simple definitions.

Scan

This activity encourages students to make a prediction about a specific piece of information that appears in the passage. The aim is to motivate students to read the passages quickly as they try to find the answer.

Reading Passage

Each reading passage in Book 3 is about 350 words. The eight units each contain three reading passages based around a common theme: the first passage is about a person, the second is about a place, and the third is about a thing. Each reading passage recycles new words from earlier passages so that students can gradually build on and consolidate their vocabulary. The language is carefully graded so that students gain confidence in reading. Each reading passage is also available on an audio CD, narrated by a native English speaker. The CD is available separately.

Which Meaning?

This feature focuses on a word in the passage that has more than one dictionary meaning. Students must choose which of the dictionary definitions fits the word as it is used in the context of the passage. The aim is to encourage students to use dictionaries more effectively and to think about the meaning of words in context.

Check Your Comprehension

These multiple-choice questions check students' understanding of the passage. The questions include key skills such as understanding the main idea, reading for details, reading for inference, and understanding text references.

Vocabulary Review

This section reviews the vocabulary presented in the unit. It includes a wide variety of activities, such as Words in Context (filling in the gaps), Sentence Completion (completing short advertisements and e-mails), and Wrong Word (finding the word that doesn't fit the group). Other activities include Word Families, Synonyms and Antonyms, True or False, and puzzles such as Crosswords, Word Searches, and Scrambled Words. The aim is to help students begin to use the new words as part of their active vocabulary.

What About You?

This section is divided into two parts: Speaking and Writing. The aim is to encourage students to use some of the new words they have learned in a more personal context. The activity can be done in pairs or in small groups.

Reading Quiz

This features a short passage—an e-mail, a letter or a short information piece—followed by six multiple choice test questions. The passage includes many of the new words from the unit. The multiple choice format and the range of question types reflect the style of questions that students will encounter in standardized tests such as the TOIEC® and TOEFL® tests. The aim of the quiz is to act as a unit test and also to help students with test preparation.

Extra Features

Vocabulary Self-Quiz

This is a unit-by-unit word list which lists the new words in each passage. It also includes space for students to write any extra words from the unit that they want to learn. There is a space next to each word where students can write a translation, or other notes, and there is also a space for them to test themselves. The aim is to help students study and review the words outside class.

Vocabulary Index

This is an index of the new vocabulary items which appear in the passages. Each item is followed by a reference to the passage where it is introduced, and also to the subsequent passages where it reappears.

Answer Key

The Answer Key is available on the OUP Website, and can be downloaded at www.oup.com/elt/teacher/peopleplacesandthings.

ACKNOWLEDGMENTS

The author and publisher would like to thank the following teachers, whose reviews, comments, and suggestions contributed to the development of *People, Places, and Things*:

Jeong Mi Choi, BCM Junior High School, Seoul, Korea; Jeremy Greenway, Shinmin Senior High School, Taichung, Taiwan; Sabrina Hsieh, Sacred Heart High School, Touliu, Taiwan; Shigeru Ichikawa, Todaiji Gakuen Junior and Senior High Schools, Nara, Japan; Tae Woo Kang, Kang Tae Woo Language School, Seoul, Korea; Josie Lai, Hsin Sheng Children's English School, Taoyuan, Taiwan; Jessie Lee, Tunghai University, Taichung, Taiwan; Masahiro Shirai, Doshisha Girls' Junior and Senior High Schools, Kyoto, Japan; Atsuko Tsuda, Keio Gijuku University, Tokyo, Japan; Arthur Tu, Taipei YMCA, Taipei, Taiwan.

In addition, the author would like to thank the following for their helpful comments and suggestions: Richard Firsten, Lindsey Hopkins Technical Education Center, Miami, Florida, U.S.A.; Maureen McCarthy, Miami Dade College, Miami, Florida, U.S.A.; Christine Meloni, Ph.D., George Washington University, Washington, DC, U.S.A.; Maureen O'Hara, Miami Dade College, Miami, Florida, U.S.A.; Katherine Rawson, Montgomery College, Montgomery, Maryland, U.S.A; Cynthia Schuemann, Miami Dade College, Miami, Florida, U.S.A.

UNIT 1

DATING

PEOPLE

PREPARE TO READ
Discuss these questions.

1. What are some ways people can find someone to date?

2. The couple in the picture met through a matchmaking service. How much do you think they paid for the service?

WORD FOCUS
Match the words with their definitions.

A.

1. average __	**a.** a famous person
2. celebrity __	**b.** what you don't like about something
3. client __	**c.** normal; usual
4. complaint __	**d.** a meeting to get professional advice
5. consultation __	**e.** a customer

B.

1. fee __	**a.** two people or things that go well together
2. insist __	**b.** say strongly
3. luxurious __	**c.** possible
4. match __	**d.** money paid for services
5. potential __	**e.** very comfortable and expensive

SCAN
A. Guess the answer. Circle *a* or *b*.

According to the book of *Guinness World Records*, Orly Hadeda

a. is the most expensive matchmaker in the world.

b. has the most famous clients in the world.

B. Scan the passage quickly to check your answer.

Orly Hadeda

One common **complaint** of the rich and famous is that they don't have time to look for love. Orly Hadeda has made a successful business out of helping these lonely
5 **celebrities** improve their romantic lives. Orly the Matchmaker, as she prefers to be called, is the daughter of a couple who made a living as matchmakers—professional marriage arrangers. Orly's approach to the business,
10 however, is a bit different from her parents'. She decided that she wasn't interested in arranging marriages between any **average** pair. Instead, she moved to Beverly Hills, California, and started a business that
15 specialized in finding love **matches** for wealthy people.

In 2003, Orly the Matchmaker was included in the book of *Guinness World Records*. She was named as the most expensive matchmaker
20 in the world. Though Orly's company is small, she spends about one million dollars a year on advertising. She can afford the costs of attracting the rich and famous because her average **client** pays around $100,000 for her

25 services. But not just anyone can hire Orly Hadeda. She doesn't accept clients who are overweight, unhealthy, or unattractive. She also **insists** that all of her male clients earn more than $250,000 dollars a year.

30 Orly meets face-to-face with all of her clients. **Potential** clients who meet her requirements fly to Beverly Hills for a personal **consultation** with her. They stay at a luxurious hotel on Rodeo Drive and dine with Orly in
35 first-<u>class</u> restaurants. The **luxurious** treatment that Orly gives her clients is all included in her **fee**. She expects her male clients to treat their female dates in a similar manner. With an old-fashioned heart, Orly believes that the
40 man should always arrange and pay for the date, even if the woman is also a millionaire. Maybe it's true that money can't buy love, but it can buy a first-class matchmaking service.

WHICH MEANING?
What does *class* mean in line 35?

1 (*noun*) lesson
2 (*noun*) level
3 (*noun*) kind

CHECK YOUR COMPREHENSION

Read the passage again and answer the questions. Circle your answers.

MAIN IDEA

1. What is this passage mainly about?
   A. A woman who runs a dating service
   B. People who live in Beverly Hills
   C. Lonely people looking for love
   D. A family of matchmakers

DETAIL

2. What kind of work did Orly's parents do?
   A. They wrote books.
   B. They were matchmakers.
   C. They owned a first-class restaurant.
   D. They ran a hotel on Rodeo Drive.

3. About how much do Orly's services normally cost?
   A. $10,000
   B. $25,000
   C. $100,000
   D. $250,000

4. What is true about the clients who meet Orly's requirements?
   A. They get a personal consultation at home.
   B. They consult with her over the Internet.
   C. They meet with her in Beverly Hills.
   D. They invite her to eat at a restaurant.

INFERENCE

5. What is true about all of Orly's clients?
   A. They are good-looking.
   B. They live in Beverly Hills.
   C. They have tried Internet dating.
   D. They read the *Guinness World Records*.

TEXT REFERENCE

6. In line 43, *but it can buy a first-class matchmaking service*, what does the word *it* refer to?
   A. An old-fashioned heart
   B. A millionaire
   C. Romance
   D. Money

PLACES

PREPARE TO READ
Discuss these questions.

1. What is the person in the photo doing?

2. Do you think a supermarket is a good place to find a date? Why or why not?

WORD FOCUS
Match the words with their definitions.

A.

1. aisle __   **a.** talk casually

2. chat __   **b.** an open space between rows of shelves or chairs

3. embellish __   **c.** cause; give an idea

4. environment __   **d.** make something more beautiful

5. inspire __   **e.** situation; things that surround you

B.

1. intention __   **a.** choose

2. location __   **b.** a place

3. phenomenon __   **c.** unsure; doubtful

4. pick out __   **d.** a purpose or plan

5. skeptical __   **e.** something unusual that happens

SCAN
A. Guess the answer. Circle *a* or *b*.

It is _____ for a single person to find a date in Paris.

a. easy   *b.* difficult

B. Scan the passage quickly to check your answer.

The Dating Supermarket

Although Paris is often considered the city of romance, close to a million adults who call it home are single. Many single people say that France's capital is one of the most difficult 5 places to meet people. The complaints of this lonely group have **inspired** a new **phenomenon** known as "supermarket dating." At Galerie Lafayette Gourmet, singles can shop for more than just the items on their grocery list. They 10 can look for someone who has blue eyes, brown hair, and is 1.8 meters tall, or whatever may be on their romantic shopping list.

At this Paris **location**, single people of all ages can schedule their shopping for Thursday 15 nights between 6:30 and 9:00 P.M. When they walk through the door, they pick up a purple basket to advertise that they are looking for love. They try to arrive early because the baskets disappear quickly, and then they 20 have to wait in line for their <u>turn</u> to wander the store **aisles**. With purple baskets in hand, shoppers can consider their romantic options while they **pick out** their groceries.

When they are ready to pay, they can go to 25 the checkout line that is especially for singles who want to **chat**.

Most of the people who look for love in the supermarket are **skeptical** of Internet dating. They know that it is too easy to **embellish** 30 one's appearance or to lie about one's age over the Internet. The supermarket, on the other hand, is considered a safe and casual **environment** in which to meet a potential match. In addition, what one finds in another's 35 grocery basket can say a thing or two about that person's character or **intentions**. Buying pet food can be a man's way of showing a potential match that he has a sensitive side. Women who fill their baskets with low-fat 40 food show their healthy style of living. These days it's possible to find much more than food at a grocery store.

WHICH MEANING?
What does *turn* mean in line 20?
1 (*noun*) bend
2 (*verb*) change
3 (*noun*) opportunity to do something

CHECK YOUR COMPREHENSION

Read the passage again and answer the questions. Circle your answers.

MAIN IDEA

1. What is this passage mainly about?
   A. Grocery shopping
   B. The best stores in Paris
   C. A place to meet potential dates
   D. The disadvantages of Internet dating

DETAIL

2. What is Galerie Lafayette Gourmet?
   A. A singles club
   B. A beauty salon
   C. A grocery store
   D. A dating service

3. What do shoppers at Galerie Lafayette Gourmet use purple baskets to do?
   A. To show that they want a date
   B. To hold a lot of groceries
   C. To look fashionable
   D. To get a discount

4. What should you do if you want to look for a date at Galerie Lafayette Gourmet?
   A. Buy pet food
   B. Shop with a friend
   C. Carry a shopping list
   D. Go shopping on Thursday evening

INFERENCE

5. According to the passage, why do people look for love in the supermarket?
   A. Because all the shoppers are good-looking
   B. Because dating services are too expensive
   C. Because it's safer than Internet dating
   D. Because it's very convenient

TEXT REFERENCE

6. In line 2, *close to a million adults who call it home are single*, what does the word *it* refer to?
   A. Paris
   B. France
   C. The area close to Paris
   D. Galerie Lafayette Gourmet

THINGS

PREPARE TO READ
Discuss these questions.

1. Who do you think can best help you find a partner—your parents or your friends?

2. Where is a good place to go on a first date?

WORD FOCUS
Match the words with their definitions.

A.

1. approximately __   **a.** cancel
2. back out __   **b.** make sure about
3. eldest __   **c.** natural feeling
4. ensure __   **d.** about; more or less
5. instinct __   **e.** oldest

B.

1. judgment __   **a.** arrive; appear
2. show up __   **b.** depend on; believe in
3. suitable __   **c.** opinion
4. trust __   **d.** not probable
5. unlikely __   **e.** good; right

SCAN

A. Guess the answer. Circle *a* or *b*.

In Korea, parents often arranged marriages for their children

a. until the 1950s.   *b.* until the 1970s.

B. Scan the passage quickly to check your answer.

The Korean 'Meeting'

For many young people in Korea, looking for love is as casual and comfortable as going out for a coffee with friends. Since the 1970s, it has been common for young men and
5 women to hold group 'meetings' for the purpose of finding a love match. Throughout Korea, <u>rows</u> of university students can be found having group dates in restaurants or cafes. These meetings allow singles to get to
10 know each other in a relaxed environment. It is common for students with the same major to arrange these meetings, ensuring at least one common interest among the group. The men and women sit across from each other
15 and change seats if a match is **unlikely**.

Though the original meetings were small in size (**approximately** four members of each sex), young people soon began to collect in much larger groups of 20 or more. Rather
20 than double or triple dates, meetings in the 1980s and later became more like sit-down singles clubs. One problem with these larger meetings is that it is much more difficult to keep the number of men and women equal.
25 In order to **ensure** that everyone has a partner, the group meeting relies on a *daeta*. This is a person that can be called at the last minute if someone **backs out** or forgets to **show up**.

The Korean meeting is quite different from
30 the traditional dating system known as *seon*. In this ancient practice, the **eldest** members of the family arranged matches for their young relatives. Before the 1970s, most marriages were formed in this way. Young people **trusted**
35 their families to make good matches for them. However, in a meeting young people had to learn to trust their own **instincts**. Young people who did not want to put their trust in family members, but who also didn't
40 trust their own **judgment**, began to ask their friends to help them find a **suitable** match. This type of dating, known as *sogaeting*, became popular in the 1990s. Matchmaking services that demand large fees have also
45 become popular in recent times.

WHICH MEANING?
What does *rows* mean in line 7?

 1 (*noun*) lines
 2 (*noun*) fights
 3 (*verb*) moves a boat using pieces of wood

CHECK YOUR COMPREHENSION

Read the passage again and answer the questions. Circle your answers.

MAIN IDEA
1. What is this passage mainly about?
  A. Korean weddings
  B. University social life
  C. A modern way to find a partner
  D. Traditional matchmaking in Korea

DETAIL
2. Who arranges Korean meetings?
  A. Parents
  B. Young people
  C. University professors
  D. The eldest family member

3. What is a *daeta*?
  A. A person who replaces another
  B. A meeting arranger
  C. A date made at a meeting
  D. A person who doesn't show up

4. What is *seon* the name for?
  A. Grandparents
  B. Family-arranged matches
  C. Friends who help you find a mate
  D. Fees paid to matchmaking services

INFERENCE
5. What do people do at a Korean meeting?
  A. They listen to a lecture about dating.
  B. They ask their grandparents for advice.
  C. They eat, drink, and have casual conversations.
  D. They conduct formal interviews of potential mates.

TEXT REFERENCE
6. In line 34, *Young people trusted their families to make good matches for them*, what does the word *them* refer to?
  A. Marriages
  B. Relatives
  C. Families
  D. Young people

VOCABULARY REVIEW

CROSSWORD PUZZLE
Complete the crossword using the clues.

Across

1. cause someone to feel or act in a new or better way

3. The child who only has younger brothers and sisters is the _____.

6. a meeting where advice is given

8. not probable

9. something that happens that people often consider odd or amazing

Down

1. natural feeling

2. a famous person

4. make something look or seem better than it really is

5. possible

7. normal

WORDS IN CONTEXT
Fill in the blanks with words from each box.

match	location	phenomenon	judgment	complaint

1. This restaurant isn't a good _____ for a date. It's too bright and noisy.

2. I think Sarah has excellent _____. She always chooses nice boys to date.

3. Robert and Martha are a really good _____. They get along so well together.

4. Looking for a date on the Internet has become a common _____.

5. The coffee wasn't hot, so I made a _____ to the restaurant manager.

celebrities	consultation	intention	environment	turn

6. My grades were not good, so I had a _____ with my teacher.

7. After I finish school, my _____ is to get a job and make a lot of money.

8. There is a long line to buy tickets. We'll have to wait our _____.

9. We saw several _____ at the party. It's so exciting to meet famous people.

10. School is a safe _____ in which to make new friends.

potential	class	inspires	row	trust

11. This warm spring weather _____ me to go outside and enjoy nature.

12. We were sitting in the last _____ of seats so we couldn't see the actors well.

13. Although it's more expensive, I prefer to buy tickets for seats in first _____.

14. I know my parents will find a good wife for me. I really _____ them.

15. You have the _____ to do well if you study more.

WORD FAMILIES
Fill in the blanks with words from each box.

luxury (*noun*)	**luxuriate** (*verb*)	**luxurious** (*adjective*)

1. _____ is important to me, so I always travel first class.

2. This is an expensive hotel, and the rooms are very _____.

insisted (*verb*)	**insistent** (*adjective*)	**insistently** (*adverb*)

3. I didn't really like the restaurant, but Susan _____ that we eat there.

4. Sam was _____ that Marina go on a date with him.

suitability (*noun*)	**suits** (*verb*)	**suitable** (*adjective*)

5. That color really _____ you; it makes you look so pretty.

6. Black isn't a _____ color to wear at a wedding.

PHRASAL VERBS
Circle the correct words.

1. I want to *show / show up* you the painting I made in my art class.

2. A lot of people *showed / showed up* for the party, and we all had a great time.

3. First Tom said he would help me with this work, but then he *backed / backed out*.

4. I tried to *back / back out* the car into the garage, but I hit the wall instead.

5. Will you help me *pick / pick out* a birthday present for my brother?

6. These apples are ripe. We can *pick / pick out* them.

SYNONYMS OR ANTONYMS?

Look at the word pairs. Are the words synonyms, antonyms, or neither?
Check the correct answer.

			Synonyms	Antonyms	Neither
1.	instinct	feeling	☐	☐	☐
2.	unlikely	probable	☐	☐	☐
3.	average	same	☐	☐	☐
4.	ensure	find	☐	☐	☐
5.	fee	money	☐	☐	☐
6.	embellish	decorate	☐	☐	☐
7.	aisle	chair	☐	☐	☐
8.	approximately	many	☐	☐	☐
9.	client	customer	☐	☐	☐
10.	eldest	youngest	☐	☐	☐
11.	skeptical	sure	☐	☐	☐
12.	chat	talk	☐	☐	☐

WHAT ABOUT YOU?
Speaking

Ask your partner these questions.

1. What time do you usually show up for school?

2. Who do you like to chat with at lunch time?

3. What do you think are suitable clothes to wear to a party?

4. Which celebrities would you like to meet?

5. What do you think is a good location for a date?

Writing

Now write about your partner. Use your partner's answers to the questions.

Example: _Tina usually shows up for school at 7:30._

1. _____

2. _____

3. _____

4. _____

5. _____

READING QUIZ

Read the passage and answer the questions. Circle your answers.

File   Edit   View   Tools   Help

Back   Forward   Stop   Refresh   Home

FIRST DATE.COM:
♥ Dating Questionnaire ♥

a. What is your intention on a first date?
- ☐ To find a love match
5 ☐ To make a friend
- ☐ To pass time
- ☐ Other

b. Which celebrity couple inspires you to find the perfect match?

10 [   ]

c. How do you pick out the clothes you are going to wear on a first date?
- ☐ I choose something suitable for the event.
- ☐ I wear my favorite clothes every time.
15 ☐ I consult a friend that I trust.
- ☐ I don't really think about it.

d. Have you ever shown up late or backed out of a date at the last minute?
- ☐ Yes   ☐ No

20 **e.** Do you insist on paying for the first date?
- ☐ Yes   ☐ No

f. How do you ensure your own personal security on a first date?
- ☐ I arrange my own ride.
25 ☐ I carry a cell phone.
- ☐ I tell a friend the location of my date.
- ☐ I follow my instinct.

g. Are you skeptical of Internet dating?
- ☐ Yes   ☐ No

30 **h.** Are you interested in a consultation* with one of our dating experts?
- ☐ Yes   ☐ No

NO FEE for first time clients!

MAIN IDEA

1. Who will fill out this questionnaire?
- **A.** Someone who is looking for a date
- **B.** Someone who wants to meet a celebrity
- **C.** Someone who needs advice about clothes
- **D.** Someone who is interested in becoming a matchmaker

DETAIL

2. Which of the following is NOT asked about?
- **A.** Internet dating
- **B.** Paying for a date
- **C.** Dating intentions
- **D.** Locations for a date

INFERENCE

3. What is free?
- **A.** The first date
- **B.** The first hour
- **C.** The first client
- **D.** The first consultation

TEXT ORGANIZATION

4. Which question asks about staying safe?
- **A.** Question d
- **B.** Question e
- **C.** Question f
- **D.** Question g

VOCABULARY

5. What does *suitable* in line 13 mean?
- **A.** Expensive
- **B.** Serious
- **C.** Pretty
- **D.** Right

6. What does *backed out* in line 17 mean?
- **A.** Canceled
- **B.** Accepted
- **C.** Dressed
- **D.** Invited

DOLPHINS

PEOPLE

a dolphin

PREPARE TO READ
Discuss these questions.

1. Why do people like dolphins?

2. What do dolphins need in order to survive in the wild?

WORD FOCUS
Match the words with their definitions.

A.

1. adapt __   **a.** a type of cage
2. captivity __   **b.** the place where an animal naturally lives
3. habitat __   **c.** in contradiction
4. ironically __   **d.** get used to
5. pen __   **e.** the opposite of freedom

B.

1. priority __   **a.** course of action
2. process __   **b.** the daily rise and fall of the sea
3. rehabilitate __   **c.** worry; tension
4. stress __   **d.** the most important thing
5. tide __   **e.** return to health

SCAN
A. Guess the answer. Circle *a* or *b*.

Flipper is the name of a

a. dolphin TV character.   ***b.*** dolphin trainer.

B. Scan the passage quickly to check your answer.

Ric O'Barry

While many people are not familiar with the name Ric O'Barry, people all over the world recognize the name of his pet dolphin, Flipper. There were actually five dolphins that shared

5 the starring role on the hit TV series, *Flipper*. When Cathy, the lead dolphin actor, died in his arms because of an illness caused by **stress** in **captivity**, O'Barry decided to put his love of dolphins to work in a new way. He created

10 the Dolphin Project, an organization that **rehabilitates** stressed dolphins and returns them to their natural **habitat**. O'Barry suggests that, like humans, no two dolphins are alike. Each dolphin that he attempts to rehabilitate

15 requires a different plan of action. Some dolphins that are born in captivity may only **adapt** to life in a sea **pen**. Others are eventually able to return to life at sea and even join their dolphin friends again.

20 From the very beginning of the rehabilitation **process**, O'Barry works to build a trusting relationship with the dolphins. In order to find out exactly what type of care each dolphin needs, O'Barry spends as much time

25 as possible with each one. He often sets up a tent and hammock for himself near the dolphin pens to provide comfort for nervous dolphins. He accompanies dolphins in transport, which is generally the most stressful step in the

30 rehabilitation process.

Teaching a dolphin how to catch live fish again is a **priority** in O'Barry's rehabilitation process. Dolphins in captivity are taught to do tricks for the reward of dead fish, so they never

35 learn how to catch their own dinner. **Ironically**, this former dolphin trainer now has the difficult task of teaching dolphins how to fish for themselves so that they can regain their independence. Other necessary <u>steps</u> include

40 reintroducing dolphins to the rhythm of the **tides** and making sure they can swim strongly enough to escape predators. All these things help ensure that a former captive dolphin can survive in its natural ocean environment.

WHICH MEANING?
What does *steps* mean in line 39?

1 (*noun*) stairs
2 (*verb*) walks
3 (*noun*) parts of a larger action

CHECK YOUR COMPREHENSION

Read the passage again and answer the questions. Circle your answers.

MAIN IDEA

1. What is the main topic of this passage?
A. A famous dolphin actor
B. A man who helps dolphins
C. Professional dolphin trainers
D. Scientists who study dolphins

DETAIL

2. Why did Cathy die?
A. She didn't know how to find food.
B. She couldn't escape a predator.
C. She was injured while acting.
D. She was unhappy in captivity.

3. What is the main goal of the Dolphin Project?
A. To teach people about the needs of dolphins
B. To help dolphins adapt to life in captivity
C. To help dolphins return to freedom
D. To train dolphins to be actors

4. According to the passage, what do dolphins need to know to survive in the wild?
A. How to attack predators
B. How to swim fast
C. How to do tricks
D. All of the above

INFERENCE

5. Why does O'Barry accompany dolphins in transport?
A. To ensure that they arrive at their destination
B. To start training them right away
C. To help them feel relaxed
D. To feed them

TEXT ORGANIZATION

6. In line 24, *O'Barry spends as much time as possible with each one*, what does the word *one* refer to?
A. Dolphin
B. Process
C. Relationship
D. Type

PLACES

a stranded dolphin

PREPARE TO READ
Discuss these questions.

1. What are some ways a wild dolphin could get injured?

2. What might you see inside a dolphin and whale hospital?

WORD FOCUS
Match the words with their definitions.

A.
1. biologist __   a. equipment
2. euthanize __   b. a scientist who studies living things
3. gear __   c. deadly
4. lethal __   d. purpose
5. mission __   e. help an ill or injured animal die

B.
1. presumably __   a. unable to leave
2. severe __   b. cutting open a body to fix a problem
3. staff __   c. probably
4. stranded __   d. employees
5. surgery __   e. very bad

SCAN
A. Guess the answer. Circle *a* or *b*.

Mote's Dolphin and Whale Hospital is in

a. Alaska.   *b.* Florida.

B. Scan the passage quickly to check your answer.

Mote's Dolphin and Whale Hospital

Every year, hundreds of **stranded** dolphins are found on beaches around the world. Although it isn't an uncommon phenomenon, scientists still are not sure why these dolphins seek dry
5 land to die. **Presumably**, they are not expecting to be rescued by humans. However, since 1994, a team of marine **biologists** at Mote's Dolphin and Whale Hospital in Florida has made it their **mission** to rehabilitate as many
10 of these stranded dolphins as possible. They are proud of their 30% success rate, as compared to the world average of 5%.

A dolphin may become stranded for a number of reasons. It may be sick and dying.
15 A shark or stingray may have attacked it. Often, people are at fault. Marine animals can get caught in fishing **gear** or become ill from polluted water. Although the first priority at Mote's is to return dolphins to
20 their natural habitat, many dolphins with **severe** injuries or diseases are given **lethal** injections right at the beach. Others are **euthanized** at the hospital if it seems that they are unlikely to get well. The Dolphin
25 and Whale Hospital's **staff** considers every

<u>case</u> a success story as long as something is learned about the species.

If it can't be in the ocean, the next best place for an ill dolphin is at a hospital like
30 Mote's. When a dolphin arrives at the hospital, it is placed in a huge tank filled with natural seawater. The tank is 30 meters wide and holds 190,000 liters of water. Several staff members join the dolphin in the tank. While
35 some take blood samples and give the dolphin medicine, others hold up the sick animal if it can't swim alone. In another part of the hospital, staff members give sick dolphins x-rays or perform **surgery** on them.

40 When dolphins show marked improvement and appear interested in life at sea, they graduate to the 750,000-liter pen. There they have more room to swim and grow strong, and the staff helps them to relearn
45 the survival skills they will need in the wild.

WHICH MEANING?
What does *case* mean in line 26?
1 (*noun*) box or bag
2 (*noun*) situation
3 (*noun*) argument

CHECK YOUR COMPREHENSION

Read the passage again and answer the questions. Circle your answers.

MAIN IDEA

1. What is this passage mainly about?
- **A.** Polluted water harming dolphins
- **B.** Doctors performing surgery on dolphins
- **C.** Scientists helping sick dolphins
- **D.** Hospital staff swimming with dolphins

DETAIL

2. How does Mote's Dolphin and Whale Hospital compare with other dolphin hospitals?
- **A.** It helps more dolphins every year.
- **B.** Its success rate is higher than the average.
- **C.** Its tanks are bigger.
- **D.** It has a larger staff.

3. Why do dolphins become stranded?
- **A.** They are sick.
- **B.** They get injured.
- **C.** Their habitat becomes polluted.
- **D.** All of the above

4. What is the highest priority at Mote's Dolphin and Whale Hospital?
- **A.** To take dolphins back to the wild
- **B.** To euthanize severely ill dolphins
- **C.** To learn more about the species
- **D.** To give dolphins medicine

INFERENCE

5. Why are stranded dolphins given lethal injections?
- **A.** There's no room for them at the hospital.
- **B.** They are too far away to return to their home.
- **C.** It's too difficult to transport them to the hospital.
- **D.** They are too sick or hurt to be cured.

TEXT REFERENCE

6. Which paragraph describes medical treatment given to dolphins?
- **A.** The first paragraph
- **B.** The second paragraph
- **C.** The third paragraph
- **D.** The fourth paragraph

THINGS

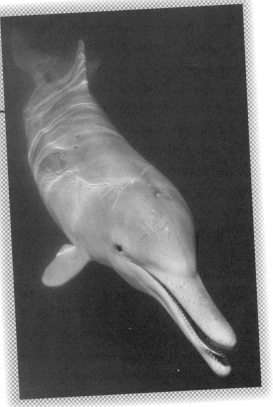

a Chinese white dolphin

PREPARE TO READ
Discuss these questions.

1. What color are dolphins?

2. What are some reasons that dolphins could become endangered?

WORD FOCUS
Match the words with their definitions.

A.
1. blush __   **a.** a picture
2. disrupt __   **b.** exist no more
3. extinction __   **c.** adulthood
4. image __   **d.** become red from embarrassment
5. maturity __   **e.** disturb

B.
1. mere __   **a.** a guess
2. navigate __   **b.** spy; find out secrets
3. reproduction __   **c.** simple; only
4. snoop __   **d.** having babies
5. theory __   **e.** find the way

SCAN
A. Guess if this is true or false. Circle *a* or *b*.
Chinese white dolphins are gray when they are born.

a. True   *b.* False

B. Scan the passage quickly to check your answer.

TRACK 7 Chinese White Dolphins

When one thinks of the colorful creatures of the sea, dolphins are not usually the first to come to mind. Though they are born dark gray like other dolphins, Chinese white dolphins
5 become pink by the time they reach **maturity**. There are a number of **theories** about why they change color over time. Some biologists believe it is because the dolphins eat shellfish. Others say it is their blood showing through
10 their skin, similar to humans when we **blush**. Their rarity has led Chinese white dolphins to become both a tourist attraction and an endangered species.

Despite the damage that has been done
15 to the western waters of Hong Kong, they are still the preferred habitat of the Chinese white dolphin. The construction of Hong Kong's Chep Lap Kok Airport in the late 1990s caused a great deal of stress for the
20 local dolphins. Their population <u>dropped</u> from a **mere** 400 or so to less than 100. While the airport was under construction, boat traffic increased, the water became polluted, and the noise **disrupted** the dolphins' ability to
25 **navigate** and communicate. Most of the baby dolphins that were born during the

construction of this airport did not survive. Since so few of these dolphins reach the age of **reproduction**, the species is in danger
30 of **extinction**.

People come from near and far to watch the playful behavior of these rare dolphins, which perform like acrobats in their natural environment. In a move known as *breeching,*
35 a dolphin jumps right out of the water, flopping back in with a gigantic splash. Though they appear to be playing, dolphins may breech in order to scare off predators, or simply to scratch an itch. Tourists also love to
40 spot Chinese white dolphins that are *spy hopping*. With this trick, dolphins come halfway out of the water in order to **snoop** around. The curiosity of humans and dolphins combined, however, creates various dangers
45 for these rare animals. Humans in their boats get too close to the dolphins. Many dolphins are injured or killed by fishing gear and boat engines.

WHICH MEANING?
What does *dropped* mean in line 20?
1 (verb) left out
2 (verb) got smaller
3 (verb) let fall from the hand

CHECK YOUR COMPREHENSION

Read the passage again and answer the questions. Circle your answers.

MAIN IDEA
1. What is this passage mainly about?
   A. Dolphin tricks
   B. Colors of dolphins
   C. Dangers for dolphins
   D. A rare and interesting dolphin

DETAIL
2. Why are Chinese white dolphins pink?
   A. They eat shellfish.
   B. They blush.
   C. Their blood is very bright.
   D. Nobody knows for sure.

3. What was a result of construction in the waters near Hong Kong?
   A. The dolphins had difficulty communicating.
   B. The dolphins disrupted work on the airport.
   C. The dolphins found another place to live.
   D. The dolphins stopped having babies.

4. Why might dolphins breech?
   A. To look around
   B. To entertain tourists
   C. To escape fishing gear
   D. To frighten their predators

INFERENCE
5. Why might dolphins sometimes get close to tourists?
   A. The dolphins are hungry.
   B. The dolphins are curious.
   C. The dolphins want to be scratched.
   D. The dolphins like the sound of boat engines.

TEXT REFERENCE
6. In line 11, *Their rarity has led Chinese white dolphins,* what does the word *Their* refer to?
   A. Biologists'
   B. Shellfish's
   C. Humans'
   D. Dolphins'

VOCABULARY REVIEW

SCRAMBLED WORDS
Unscramble the words to complete the sentences.

1. Dolphins often experience stress in _____. (**tactviyip**)

2. A good place to _____ a dolphin is in a sea pen. (**behailtiaetr**)

3. _____, the dolphins became stranded because of water pollution. (**ypeusablmr**)

4. Curious dolphins love to _____ on passing tourists. (**poosn**)

5. Boat traffic can disturb a dolphin's ability to _____. (**gnavieat**)

6. Because of a mere fishing net, the dolphin needed major _____. (**gsreryu**)

7. Preventing dolphin extinction is a _____ of many biologists. (**imsions**)

8. Severely injured dolphins are sometimes given _____ injections. (**eltalh**)

9. Dolphins start having babies at the age of _____. (**ceprroduntio**)

10. _____, the same man who used to catch dolphins now fights to set them free. (**roinialcly**)

WORDS IN CONTEXT
Fill in the blanks with words from each box.

extinction	adapt	gear	blushed	stranded

1. It can be difficult to _____ to a new situation, such as a new school or job.

2. Fishing can be an inexpensive and simple sport. It doesn't require a lot of _____.

3. Amanda _____ when Bob gave her the flowers.

4. Some dolphin species are in danger of _____. It will be very sad if they disappear.

5. When their boat ran out of gas, they were _____ on an island.

tide	euthanize	mere	step	image

6. When the horse unfortunately broke its leg, we had to _____ it.

7. James is a really fast reader. It took him a _____ two days to read that entire book.

8. The beach looks really small right now because the _____ is high.

9. I've never seen Hawaii, but I have an _____ of it in my mind.

10. I've finished writing my composition. The next _____ is to check for mistakes.

process	case	reproduction	snoop	priority

11. _____ among these dolphins is going up. A lot of babies were born this year.

12. Studying hard is my _____. Nothing else in my life is as important as that.

13. Stop asking so many questions. It isn't polite to _____.

14. The doctors don't treat all the sick dolphins alike. Each _____ is different.

15. Rehabilitating a stressed dolphin is a long _____. It takes many steps.

WORD FAMILIES
Fill in the blanks with words from each box.

presume (*verb*)	**presumable** (*adjective*)	**presumably** (*adverb*)

1. I don't know why Mr. Roberts isn't here today. I _____ he is sick.

2. _____ he went to the doctor.

navigator (*noun*)	**navigate** (*verb*)	**navigable** (*adjective*)

3. This river isn't _____. It's very rocky, and the water is shallow.

4. In the old days, sailors used to _____ by the stars.

severity (*noun*)	**severe** (*adjective*)	**severely** (*adverb*)

5. The dolphin was _____ ill, so they had to euthanize it.

6. Because of the _____ of my grandfather's illness, he had to spend weeks in the hospital.

WRONG WORD
One word in each group does not fit. Circle the word.

1. doctor	court	surgery	hospital
2. disrupt	interrupt	assist	disturb
3. add	decrease	drop	reduce
4. childhood	youth	maturity	birthday
5. theory	guess	fact	possibility
6. freedom	cage	captivity	lock
7. staff	workers	clients	employees
8. biologist	artist	chemist	scientist

SENTENCE COMPLETION
Complete the information sheet with words from the box.

habitat	mission	stress	rehabilitate	pens

Welcome to the Island Dolphin Hospital!

Our main job at the hospital is to _____ dolphins. We do all we can to bring them back to health. Our goal is to return healthy dolphins to their natural _____. The ocean is the best place for dolphins to live. Recovering dolphins live in sea _____ while they relearn survival skills. We cannot allow visitors in this area as it would cause too much _____ for the dolphins. They are still ill, and we want them to get better—not worse. If you would like to help us in our _____ to return these dolphins to the ocean, you can make a donation. Gifts of all sizes are accepted and appreciated.

WHAT ABOUT YOU?
Speaking
Ask your partner these questions.

1. What is a priority in your life?

2. What is something that causes stress for you?

3. Name some wild animals you have seen in captivity.

4. Name some wild animals you have seen in their natural habitat.

5. What can you see at the beach at low tide?

Writing
Now write about your partner. Use your partner's answers to the questions.
Example: Getting good grades is a priority in Lee's life.

1. _____

2. _____

3. _____

4. _____

5. _____

READING QUIZ

Read the passage and answer the questions. Circle your answers.

NOTICE TO ALL BOATERS:

Please be aware that a dolphin pen has been placed at the far end of Victoria Harbor for the purpose of rehabilitating six young dolphins that became stranded on a nearby beach last month. It is believed that one of the dolphins got caught in some fishing gear and other members of the group followed
5 him to shore. A seventh dolphin was given a lethal injection at the beach after staff attempted emergency surgery. (This dolphin, ironically named Jaws by The Marine Mission staff, had severe bite wounds, presumably from sharks in the area.)

    Rather than holding these rare Chinese white dolphins in captivity, local
10 biologists have built this pen in hopes that the animals might adapt to the natural tides of the ocean and return to the deep waters once again. The Marine Mission team asks that you please turn off your engines when nearing the pen. The sound of a mere single-engine boat can cause the animals great stress and disrupt their navigational instincts. The priority of The Marine
15 Mission is to help these dolphins reach the age of maturity and to encourage the reproduction of a species that is at risk of extinction.

MAIN IDEA

1. What is the purpose of this notice?
   - **A.** To describe the habits of wild dolphins
   - **B.** To explain how to care for sick dolphins
   - **C.** To ask for money for The Marine Mission
   - **D.** To inform boaters about the dolphins in the pen

DETAIL

2. What are boaters asked to do?
   - **A.** Help The Marine Mission care for the dolphins
   - **B.** Keep their boats quiet near the dolphin pen
   - **C.** Guide the dolphins back to the ocean
   - **D.** Be careful with their fishing gear

INFERENCE

3. What do local biologists want to do?
   - **A.** Keep the dolphins in captivity
   - **B.** Perform surgery on all the dolphins
   - **C.** Swim in the ocean with the dolphins
   - **D.** Help the dolphins return to their natural habitat

TEXT REFERENCE

4. In line 4, *other members of the group followed him to shore,* what does the word *him* refer to?
   - **A.** A fisherman
   - **B.** A biologist
   - **C.** A dolphin
   - **D.** A boater

VOCABULARY

5. What does *pen* in line 1 mean?
   - **A.** Hospital
   - **B.** Cage
   - **C.** Show
   - **D.** Boat

6. What does *severe* in line 7 mean?
   - **A.** Serious
   - **B.** Bloody
   - **C.** Round
   - **D.** Small

SOCCER

PEOPLE

David Beckham

PREPARE TO READ
Discuss these questions.

1. What do you know about David Beckham?

2. Why do you think he is so popular?

WORD FOCUS
Match the words with their definitions.

A.

1. convince __   **a.** different; individual
2. distinct __   **b.** bother
3. faze __   **c.** TV, radio, newspapers
4. heighten __   **d.** change someone's mind
5. media __   **e.** make bigger or greater

B.

1. outshine __   **a.** a representative
2. penalty __   **b.** do better than
3. spokesperson __   **c.** punishment
4. trend __   **d.** crazy; enthusiastic
5. wild __   **e.** a fashion

SCAN

A. Guess the answer. Circle *a* or *b*.

How old was David Beckham when he became a professional soccer player?

a. 18   *b.* 21

B. Scan the passage quickly to check your answer.

David Beckham

Soccer fans are crazy about their favorite teams. They are even **wilder** about their favorite players. One of the most popular soccer players in the world is David Beckham.

5 He is so famous that even people who don't <u>follow</u> soccer know his name. Beckham became a celebrity because he is one of a kind. He has talent, passion, and a **distinct** image that people can't get enough of.

10 David Beckham has always had a passion for soccer (or football, as it is known in his country, England). As a boy, he dreamed about playing for Manchester United. In 1991, his wish came true when he qualified

15 for United's junior team. Beckham's team won the Football Association Youth Cup in his first season. The next year, when he was only 18 years old, he became a professional player. By **outshining** the other players on

20 his team, Beckham landed the role of team captain. Fans and teammates were amazed by how well he took **penalty** kicks and how far he could kick the ball. Scoring a goal from the halfway line proved that he

25 deserved to be the highest-paid soccer player in the world. Changing teams from Manchester United to Real Madrid only **heightened** Beckham's popularity.

One of the reasons people love David
30 Beckham is because he is not afraid to show his true self. Appearing in public in a sarong or with painted nails does not seem to **faze** him. While many celebrities try to hide from the **media**, Beckham loves to experiment with
35 fashion in the public eye. His hair and fashion styles have set **trends** all over the world. After the 2002 World Cup, there were blond Mohawks throughout Korea. When Beckham shaved off half of an eyebrow, many young
40 people did the same thing. In Japan, one company made a three-meter-high chocolate statue of Beckham and **convinced** him to be their **spokesperson**. There are other sides to Beckham's personality, too. Many fans love the
45 fact that he is also a dedicated father: he and his wife, Victoria, have three children.

WHICH MEANING?
What does *follow* mean in line 6?
1 (*verb*) walk behind
2 (*verb*) be a fan of
3 (*verb*) understand

CHECK YOUR COMPREHENSION

Read the passage again and answer the questions. Circle your answers.

MAIN IDEA

1. What is this passage mainly about?
   A. David Beckham's family
   B. David Beckham's fashion styles
   C. Manchester United
   D. A popular soccer player

DETAIL

2. What did Beckham do in 1991?
   A. He started playing for Manchester United's junior team.
   B. He became a professional soccer player.
   C. He joined the Real Madrid team.
   D. He became team captain.

3. How has Beckham experimented with fashion?
   A. He painted his nails.
   B. He shaved off half an eyebrow.
   C. He wore a blond Mohawk.
   D. All of the above

4. What did a Japanese company do?
   A. It sold chocolate soccer balls.
   B. It asked Beckham to be its representative.
   C. It convinced Beckham to dye his hair blond.
   D. It sold tickets to the 2002 World Cup games.

INFERENCE

5. What is probably true about David Beckham?
   A. He's very shy.
   B. He never has fun.
   C. He enjoys attention.
   D. He's a follower, not a leader.

TEXT ORGANIZATION

6. In line 39, *many young people did the same thing*, what do the words *the same thing* refer to?
   A. Playing soccer
   B. Shaving off half of an eyebrow
   C. Wearing a blond Mohawk
   D. Watching Beckham in the World Cup

PLACES

PREPARE TO READ
Discuss these questions.

1. What is your favorite sport? What do you like about it?

2. Where and when do you think people began to play soccer?

WORD FOCUS
Match the words with their definitions.

A.

1. debate __   **a.** not allow

2. establish __   **b.** rule; manage

3. govern __   **c.** create

4. obsessed __   **d.** an argument

5. outlaw __   **e.** passionate about

B.

1. remotely __   **a.** a person who watches a game

2. soldier __   **b.** distantly; only a little bit

3. spectator __   **c.** make someone fall

4. trip __   **d.** a prize for winning a game

5. trophy __   **e.** a fighter

SCAN
A. Guess the answer. Circle *a* or *b*.

When did soccer become an Olympic sport?

a. 1908   *b.* 1930

B. Scan the passage quickly to check your answer.

TRACK 9 Where Did Soccer Originate?

There is great **debate** over when the first soccer game was played. Many historians believe that the first games involving kicking a ball were played by Chinese **soldiers** during
5 the Han Dynasty over 2,000 years ago. A similar game was played in Japan, Greece, and Rome. In some cultures, the ball symbolized the sun. The purpose of the game was to capture "the sun" and ensure a good growing season.

10   In medieval times, the European version only **remotely** resembled the game of soccer that exists today. It was much more violent in nature, and involved two teams, each one as large as an entire town or community.
15 Historical records show that soccer was sometimes even played with a human head. **Tripping** and biting were also allowed. Before the 1800s, the game was **outlawed** throughout much of England. The penalty for
20 playing soccer was time in jail.

     In the 1800s, students in England's colleges and universities became **obsessed** with the game once again. This time, rules were **established** to keep control over the violence
25 and the size of the teams. However, every school had its own rules, which made it hard for them to compete against each other. The Football Association was established in 1863 in order to set down rules and **govern** the
30 matches between the different teams. Six years later, the game officially became a "no hands" sport.

     The sport also gained popularity in the British navy. Sailors brought their soccer balls
35 on board and played the game in their free time. Young people around the world showed up to watch the sailors play and then went home and organized their own teams. By the twentieth century, the whole world was playing
40 soccer. In 1908, soccer became an Olympic sport. This helped make soccer the most popular **spectator** sport in the world. The first World Cup was held in 1930 in South America. Every four years, the <u>top</u> professionals
45 compete to bring home the World Cup **trophy**.

WHICH MEANING?
What does *top* mean in line 44?
1 (*adjective*) best
2 (*verb*) do better than
3 (*noun*) cover or lid

CHECK YOUR COMPREHENSION

Read the passage again and answer the questions. Circle your answers.

MAIN IDEA

1. What is this passage mainly about?
   A. Soccer in the British navy
   B. Ancient soccer games
   C. The history of soccer
   D. The rules of soccer

DETAIL

2. What was soccer like in medieval Europe?
   A. It was very similar to modern soccer.
   B. It was a game for soldiers.
   C. It was a very violent game.
   D. It was played only in jails.

3. What happened in 1863?
   A. An organization was started to govern soccer games.
   B. A large fight broke out between soccer teams.
   C. Colleges and universities outlawed soccer.
   D. British sailors established a soccer team.

4. Where was the first World Cup held?
   A. Europe
   B. South America
   C. Greece
   D. China

INFERENCE

5. When was the "no hands" rule established?
   A. By the British universities in 1863
   B. By the Football Association in 1869
   C. By the Olympic Committee in 1908
   D. By the World Cup in 1930

TEXT REFERENCE

6. Which paragraph mentions a connection between ball games and farming?
   A. The first paragraph
   B. The second paragraph
   C. The third paragraph
   D. The fourth paragraph

THINGS

the World Cup trophy

PREPARE TO READ
Discuss these questions.

1. Do you have a favorite soccer team? Have they ever won the World Cup?

2. Which soccer team won the World Cup trophy most recently? Do you think the trophy is beautiful?

WORD FOCUS
Match the words with their definitions.

A.

1. break into ___   **a.** an exhibit; things to look at
2. conduct ___   **b.** keep
3. display ___   **c.** enter with the purpose of stealing things
4. hold on to ___   **d.** not living
5. inanimate ___   **e.** perform; carry out

B.

1. ransom ___   **a.** a copy
2. replica ___   **b.** winning
3. sculptor ___   **c.** exciting and full of activity
4. victory ___   **d.** a person who makes statues
5. whirlwind ___   **e.** money paid to kidnappers

SCAN
A. Guess the answer. Circle *a* or *b*.

In which South American country was the first World Cup competition held?

a. Brazil   *b.* Uruguay

B. Scan the passage quickly to check your answer.

THE WORLD CUP TROPHY

For an **inanimate** <u>object</u>, the Jules Rimet World Cup trophy has had a **whirlwind** of a life. French **sculptor** Abel Lafleur created the first trophy. It was named for Jules Rimet,
5 the man who established the World Cup competition. The trophy was a statue of a goddess of **victory** and was introduced at the first World Cup competition in Uruguay in 1930. During World War II, the Italian vice
10 president of FIFA (The International Football Association) hid the trophy under his bed in order to keep it out of the hands of the Nazis.

Although it survived the war, the Jules Rimet trophy was stolen from a **display** case
15 in England just before the World Cup of 1966. Like a regular kidnapping, a **ransom** demand followed, and a nationwide search for the trophy was **conducted**. A pet owner collected the reward of over $4,000 when his dog,
20 Pickles, found the trophy while snooping under a bush. The dog became a national hero and was given several awards, including a role in a film and a year's supply of dog food.

After winning the World Cup three times in
25 a row, the Brazilian Football Association was given the trophy to keep. However, on December 19, 1983, three thieves **broke into** an office in Rio de Janeiro, tied up a night watchman, and disappeared with the Jules
30 Rimet trophy. The trophy was never found again, though police found evidence that it had been melted down for gold. A **replica** was created and presented to Brazil a year later.

In 1974 FIFA held a competition for a new
35 World Cup trophy design. Italian sculptor Silvio Gazzaniga was chosen for his simple yet powerful image of two athletes holding up the world. The statue symbolizes the emotions that overcome a team in the moment of victory.
40 The tradition of giving the cup away is no longer practiced. FIFA **holds on to** this trophy and provides a replica to the winner of each World Cup. A new trophy will need to be designed after the 2038 World Cup, when the
45 base will have no more room for winning names.

WHICH MEANING?
What does *object* mean in line 1?
1 (*noun*) purpose
2 (*verb*) disagree
3 (*noun*) thing

CHECK YOUR COMPREHENSION

Read the passage again and answer the questions. Circle your answers.

MAIN IDEA

1. Which is the best title for this passage?
A. Kidnapped!
B. The History of FIFA
C. Brazil, the Winning Team
D. The Adventures of a Trophy

DETAIL

2. Who designed the first World Cup trophy?
A. Jules Rimet
B. Abel Lafleur
C. Silvio Gazzaniga
D. David Beckham

3. Where was the trophy during World War II?
A. In Brazil
B. In the hands of the Nazis
C. In a display case in England
D. In the house of the vice president of FIFA

4. What happened to the dog, Pickles, after he found the lost trophy?
A. He won $4,000.
B. He acted in a movie.
C. He attended a World Cup game.
D. He was sold by his owner for a lot of money.

INFERENCE

5. Why does FIFA no longer give the trophy to the winning team?
A. To prevent jealousy among the teams
B. To allow many people to see it
C. To protect it from thieves
D. To save money

TEXT ORGANIZATION

6. Which paragraph describes a robbery in Brazil?
A. The first paragraph
B. The second paragraph
C. The third paragraph
D. The fourth paragraph

VOCABULARY REVIEW

CROSSWORD PUZZLE
Complete the crossword using the clues.

Across

2. increase
3. items for viewing
5. very slightly
6. make illegal
8. do much better than others
9. an event that happens surprisingly fast

Down

1. punishment in sports
4. a person who watches a sport
5. a payoff to a criminal
7. a fashion

WORDS IN CONTEXT
Fill in the blanks with words from each box.

distinct	top	wild	tripped	conducted

1. I'm a big tennis fan. I'm really _____ about the sport.
2. After the bank robbery, the police _____ a search, but they never found the thief.
3. Sue is one of the _____ students in her class. She always gets excellent grades.
4. Roger has a _____ personality. There aren't many people like him.
5. Alice broke her leg when she _____ over a soccer ball.

follow	convince	established	faze	debate

6. Jane had to speak in front of the entire school, but it didn't _____ her.
7. I'm not very interested in soccer. In fact, I don't _____ any sports.
8. This school is quite old. It was _____ over 300 years ago.
9. There is great _____ about school uniforms. Not everyone agrees that students should wear them.
10. Lou really needed money, but he couldn't _____ anyone to lend him some.

spokespeople	media	objects	spectators	victory

11. You can see several interesting _____ in that display case.

12. When the soccer player made a goal, all the _____ cheered.

13. Some celebrities don't like attention from the _____. They don't want to appear in newspapers.

14. After winning the game, the players had a party to celebrate their _____.

15. Celebrities often act as _____ for companies.

WORD FAMILIES
Fill in the blanks with words from each box.

obsession (*noun*)	obsess (*verb*)	obsessed (*adjective*)

1. Some people are really _____ with soccer. They spend all their free time playing it.

2. Video games are a big _____ for many kids.

government (*noun*)	governor (*noun*)	governed (*verb*)

3. The _____ of this province lives in a big house in the capital city.

4. One political party _____ the country for fifteen years.

sculpture (*noun*)	sculptor (*noun*)	sculpt (*verb*)

5. There is a very beautiful stone _____ in the middle of the garden.

6. It was made by a well-known _____.

TRUE OR FALSE?
Are the following sentences true or false? Circle your answers.

1. A trophy is given as a penalty.	TRUE	FALSE
2. Soldiers fight in wars.	TRUE	FALSE
3. A replica of a trophy looks like the original.	TRUE	FALSE
4. Inanimate things breathe and eat.	TRUE	FALSE
5. A soccer player is an example of a spectator.	TRUE	FALSE
6. A sculptor makes statues.	TRUE	FALSE
7. Kidnappers usually ask for a ransom.	TRUE	FALSE

PHRASAL VERBS
Circle the correct words.

1. My new car is quite big. It can *hold / hold on to* eight passengers.

2. It isn't a good idea to sell your old car. I think you should *hold / hold on to* it.

3. Some thieves *broke / broke into* the jewelry store and took several diamond necklaces.

4. These cups are very delicate. Please don't *break / break into* them.

5. Look at these old books from my childhood. I've *held / held on to* them for years.

6. He kicked the soccer ball toward the house, and it *broke / broke into* a window.

WHAT ABOUT YOU?
Speaking
Ask your partner these questions.

1. Which sports do you follow?

2. Who is your favorite top athlete?

3. Which movie stars are you wild about?

4. Where do you keep your valuable objects?

5. What is something that you have held on to since you were young?

Writing
Now write about your partner. Use your partner's answers to the questions.
Example: <u>Sherry follows basketball and baseball</u>.

1. _____

2. _____

3. _____

4. _____

5. _____

READING QUIZ

Read the passage and answer the questions. Circle your answers.

Soccer: What's On the Web

It's no secret that soccer fans become obsessed with their favorite teams. In fact, soccer crowds have been known to go wild at times, resulting in the injury
5 and death of many spectators. Aggression among fans often heightens when a referee calls a bad penalty or when one team is ensured a victory. Similarly, if a celebrity like David
10 Beckham gets tripped without a referee noticing, a peaceful game can quickly turn into a war zone.

On the Website *No Violence*, Leonardo Scheinkman tries to convince
15 fans that soccer is just a game. When Leonardo was a child, his parents noticed a trend in soccer violence and debated whether or not Brazil's stadiums were a safe place to bring their kids to.
20 The family decided it was safer to watch the games on TV. This experience only remotely resembled that of watching soccer live. Remembering the disappointment of his childhood,
25 Leonardo established a Website to remind fans that soccer and violence don't go together. The pictures on his Website display an important truth about the game of soccer: a human life
30 is more important than an inanimate thing such as a trophy or a victory.

MAIN IDEA

1. What is the purpose of this passage?
   A. To describe an interesting Website
   B. To report on a violent soccer game
   C. To explain the history of soccer
   D. To talk about famous soccer players

DETAIL

2. According to the passage, what can be a cause of aggression at soccer games?
   A. The presence of a celebrity soccer player
   B. A stadium that is too small
   C. Calling a bad penalty
   D. All of the above

3. What does Leonardo Scheinkman do?
   A. He plays professional soccer.
   B. He runs an anti-violence Website.
   C. He is a security guard at a Brazilian stadium.
   D. He works as a soccer referee.

INFERENCE

4. According to the passage, what did Leonardo Scheinkman want to do as a child?
   A. Attend live soccer games
   B. Meet David Beckham
   C. Win a soccer trophy
   D. Get a better TV

VOCABULARY

5. What does *debated* in line 18 mean?
   A. Agreed
   B. Argued
   C. Decided
   D. Explained

6. What does *established* in line 25 mean?
   A. Looked for
   B. Borrowed
   C. Bought
   D. Started

BEAUTY

PEOPLE

Cindy Jackson

PREPARE TO READ
Discuss these questions.

1. What are some things people do to look more beautiful?

2. Which of those things do you think the woman in the photo has done?

WORD FOCUS
Match the words with their definitions.

A.
1. cosmetic __   **a.** exciting and attractive
2. everlasting __   **b.** related to beauty
3. fantasy __   **c.** money or property left to you by a relative
4. glamorous __   **d.** permanent
5. inheritance __   **e.** a dream

B.
1. principle __   **a.** a search
2. quest __   **b.** paint a picture on the skin
3. sag __   **c.** a complete change
4. tattoo __   **d.** an idea; a rule
5. transformation __   **e.** hang down

SCAN
A. Guess if this is true or false. Circle *a* or *b*.
Cindy Jackson was an art student.

a. True   *b.* False

B. Scan the passage quickly to check your answer.

Cindy Jackson

When Cindy Jackson was 32 years old, she wrote a list of all the things she wanted to change about her appearance. Her obsession with beauty had begun years earlier when she
5 was a farm girl in Ohio. At the age of six, she received a doll as a gift. She invented a **glamorous** life for her doll, and she fantasized about having the same sort of life herself. When she looked at herself in the mirror, the
10 image she saw wasn't ugly, but it was far from her glamorous **fantasies**. In high school, she felt that the prettier girls got all the attention and that no one noticed her.

Jackson was tired of feeling <u>plain</u> and
15 unnoticed. In 1988, she wrote her beauty wish list. She based it in part on the **principles** of beauty she had learned as an art student. She never dreamed that she would really be able to make any of these changes. But,
20 soon after writing the list, she received a small **inheritance**. It was enough to begin her **transformation** to beauty.

Jackson felt that her nose was too big and her lips were too thin. In addition, her skin

25 **sagged** in certain areas because she had lost weight. In order to solve these problems, Jackson had several surgical operations. She had surgery to remove fat from her thighs and abdomen, as well as two nose operations
30 and a face and jaw lift. Chemical peels made her skin appear brand new, and permanent makeup, including eyeliner and lipstick, was **tattooed** onto her face for an **everlasting** fresh appearance. Nine operations later, a
35 doll had come to life.

Jackson's transformation through **cosmetic** surgery has made her into a celebrity. She has written many articles describing her experience, as well as her life story entitled *Living Doll*. She
40 also acts as a cosmetic surgery consultant. Her mission is to help others achieve the same success she has in the **quest** for beauty. Jackson is now proud to say that she has made every single change that she wrote on her wish
45 list in 1988.

WHICH MEANING?

What does *plain* mean in line 14?

1 (*adjective*) not decorated
2 (*adjective*) not beautiful
3 (*adjective*) easy to understand

CHECK YOUR COMPREHENSION

Read the passage again and answer the questions. Circle your answers.

MAIN IDEA

1. What is this passage mainly about?
  A. A woman who plays with dolls
  B. A woman who is obsessed with beauty
  C. A woman who became a cosmetic surgeon
  D. A woman who is a professional makeup artist

DETAIL

2. When did Jackson make her beauty wish list?
  A. At age six
  B. In high school
  C. In art school
  D. At age 32

3. Why didn't Cindy Jackson like her nose?
  A. It was very large.
  B. It was too thin.
  C. It sagged.
  D. It was plain.

4. Cindy Jackson used _____ to remove fat from her thighs and abdomen.
  A. diets
  B. pills
  C. surgery
  D. exercise

INFERENCE

5. In high school, Jackson
  A. felt very pretty.
  B. thought she was plain.
  C. got a lot of attention.
  D. had a glamorous life.

TEXT REFERENCE

6. Which paragraph mentions a book that Cindy Jackson wrote?
  A. The first paragraph
  B. The second paragraph
  C. The third paragraph
  D. The fourth paragraph

Telesforo Iacobelli

PREPARE TO READ
Discuss these questions.

1. Do you think the man in the photo is attractive?

2. What kinds of problems do you think unattractive people might have?

WORD FOCUS
Match the words with their definitions.

A.
1. bearable __
2. elect __
3. financial __
4. genuine __
5. grade __

   a. choose by voting
   b. related to money
   c. real
   d. acceptable
   e. place in a level

B.
1. pressure __
2. prized __
3. self-proclaimed __
4. standard __
5. virtue __

   a. valued; respected
   b. self-named
   c. a good quality
   d. understood as normal by most people
   e. stress; difficulty

SCAN
A. Guess the answer. Circle *a* or *b*.

The World Capital of Ugly People is in

a. France.   *b.* Italy.

B. Scan the passage quickly to check your answer.

TRACK 12 The Ugly Capital of the World

Italy is one country where beauty is **prized** more than any other **virtue**. That is, except in the small town of Piobbico, the **self-proclaimed** World Capital of Ugly People. The
5 road sign at the edge of the town even warns visitors that they are entering the ugly zone. People who consider themselves ugly have been gathering in Piobbico since the 1960s. That's when Ugly Club president Telesforo
10 Iacobelli established a dating agency for women who believed they were too ugly to attract husbands. Iacobelli believes that he is ugly himself because he has a short nose in a country where long or large noses have
15 always been considered beautiful.

People from around the world travel to Piobbico to tell their sad stories of ugliness. During the annual Festival of the Ugly, which occurs on the first Sunday of every
20 September, hundreds of people gather in Piobbico's town <u>square</u> to **elect** the president of the Ugly Club. Iacobelli wins the election every year. The Ugly Club has over 20,000 members. They carry ID cards that **grade**
25 their ugliness from **bearable** to extreme.

A prize is awarded to Ugly Club members who qualify as extremely ugly.

The Ugly Club president insists that ugliness is a virtue. Since beautiful people get a lot of
30 attention for their beauty alone, they have to work hard to prove their other virtues. Ugly people, on the other hand, are **genuine** and don't have to prove anything to anybody, according to Iacobelli.

35 Iacobelli is a spokesperson for ugly people everywhere. He believes that the uglier one is, the better life can be. Though the club enjoys making fun of beauty, especially beauty contests, Iacobelli has a serious side as well.
40 He believes that too many people suffer from **financial** and emotional **pressures** because they don't meet society's **standards** of beauty. The fact that beautiful people are more successful in the workforce is a problem that
45 Iacobelli has attempted to bring forward to the Italian public and government.

WHICH MEANING?
What does *square* mean in line 21?

1 (*noun*) four-sided shape
2 (*adjective*) fair
3 (*noun*) plaza or small park

CHECK YOUR COMPREHENSION

Read the passage again and answer the questions. Circle your answers.

MAIN IDEA

1. What is this passage mainly about?
   A. A town where everyone is ugly
   B. A town where most women can't find husbands
   C. A town where ugly people are appreciated
   D. A town where beauty is the most important virtue

DETAIL

2. Who is Telesforo Iacobelli?
   A. The president of the Ugly Club
   B. The founder of a dating agency
   C. A spokesperson for ugly people
   D. All of the above

3. What happens on the first Sunday of September in Piobbico?
   A. Ugly Club members elect a club president.
   B. A new sign is placed at the edge of town.
   C. Ugly Club members receive new ID cards.
   D. The town dating agency sponsors a festival.

4. About how many members does the Ugly Club have?
   A. Two hundred
   B. Two thousand
   C. Twenty thousand
   D. Twenty million

INFERENCE

5. According to the passage, what is a problem for beautiful people?
   A. Their other good qualities often go unnoticed.
   B. Their beauty causes emotional difficulties.
   C. They aren't as successful as ugly people at work.
   D. They often suffer from financial problems.

TEXT ORGANIZATION

6. Which paragraph describes the activities of the Ugly Club?
   A. The first paragraph
   B. The second paragraph
   C. The third paragraph
   D. The fourth paragraph

THINGS

PREPARE TO READ
Discuss these questions.

1. What kinds of beauty products do women use?

2. What kinds of beauty products do men use?

WORD FOCUS
Match the words with their definitions.

A.
1. appropriate __   **a.** promise
2. dye __   **b.** womanly
3. essential __   **c.** change the color of something
4. feminine __   **d.** necessary
5. guarantee __   **e.** correct; suitable

B.
1. marketing __   **a.** aim at
2. masculine __   **b.** advertise a product
3. promote __   **c.** manly
4. reluctant __   **d.** not wanting to do something
5. target __   **e.** finding an audience that will buy a product

SCAN
A. Guess the answer. Circle *a* or *b*.

Male beauty products have been fashionable since

a. the 1970s.   *b.* the 1990s.

B. Scan the passage quickly to check your answer.

TRACK 13

Male Beauty Products

For years, cosmetic companies have been telling women that beauty is a secret to success. Now these companies are **targeting** men, too. Men are being pressured to pay more attention to
5 their appearance in order to improve their personal and professional lives. Since the late 1990s, the male trend has been to smell, look, and feel beautiful, even if that means **dying** one's hair and putting on makeup.

10   **Appropriate marketing** of male beauty products is **essential**. Since beauty products have traditionally been considered **feminine**, men need to know that there are products especially designed for them. Companies which
15 have never had a connection with products for women have been among the most successful. Products that **guarantee** natural ingredients and a natural look attract male buyers. Products that recognize a man's interest in sports are
20 also successful. By hiring spokespeople with a **masculine** image, such as David Beckham, cosmetic companies have been able to convince men that it's okay to be beautiful. One well-known company relies on male

25 athletes to **promote** its skin care products.

The male beauty industry first introduced products such as aftershave, cologne, and hair dye, and then moved into areas usually considered feminine, such as skin care and
30 makeup. Products that guarantee hair growth for bald men and dyes that cover gray hair have grown in popularity around the world. Men in general have become interested in cosmetic products that can help them look
35 younger, fitter, and more handsome. Even those who may be **reluctant** to ask for advice from female beauty consultants now have more choices. Many large department stores have opened male beauty departments
40 <u>run</u> by male cosmeticians. Now men can get cosmetic advice and buy cosmetic products in an environment that feels masculine. The quest for beauty is no longer just for women.

WHICH MEANING?
What does *run* mean in line 40?
1 (*verb*) manage
2 (*verb*) go faster than walking
3 (*verb*) continue

CHECK YOUR COMPREHENSION

Read the passage again and answer the questions. Circle your answers.

MAIN IDEA

1. What is this passage mainly about?
  A. A new beauty trend
  B. Places to buy cosmetics
  C. How companies advertise products
  D. The biggest cosmetic companies

DETAIL

2. According to the passage, what kind of products do men like to use?
  A. Products that smell beautiful
  B. Products that have natural ingredients
  C. Products that are designed for women
  D. Products that come in attractive packages

3. Why do some cosmetic companies hire athletes to promote their products?
  A. Athletes usually look natural.
  B. Athletes have a masculine image.
  C. Athletes often use cosmetic products.
  D. Athletes don't charge a lot of money for this work.

4. According to the passage, which of the following is a product that men buy?
  A. Hair dye
  B. Nail polish
  C. Eyeliner
  D. Lipstick

INFERENCE

5. According to the passage, what must companies that sell cosmetics to men do?
  A. Sell their products mostly in department stores
  B. Keep the prices of their products low
  C. Make sure their products don't seem feminine
  D. Hire beauty consultants to promote their products

TEXT REFERENCE

6. In line 13, *there are products especially designed for them*, what does the word *them* refer to?
  A. Men
  B. Women
  C. Products
  D. Companies

VOCABULARY REVIEW

WORD SEARCH

Find and circle the vocabulary below. Then look for a word in the first line of the puzzle to complete this movie title: "_____ and the Beast."

bearable
cosmetic
essential
feminine
prized
sag
standard
tattoo
transformation
virtue

Y	T	U	A	E	B	N	R	L	F	B	O	W	F	S
B	U	E	T	K	K	O	A	X	E	E	O	W	A	M
J	U	T	H	T	N	I	S	L	M	A	T	G	B	B
V	Z	Y	A	K	T	T	D	B	I	R	T	I	X	N
V	P	M	Z	N	A	A	X	E	N	A	A	S	N	R
T	M	C	E	N	T	M	T	H	I	B	T	S	B	F
R	F	S	D	T	Y	R	C	F	N	L	P	X	U	G
H	S	A	S	B	K	O	C	I	E	E	Y	S	W	V
E	R	M	A	J	Z	F	H	C	T	P	K	C	X	N
D	S	J	Z	W	B	S	I	M	T	E	N	U	P	D
P	R	I	Z	E	D	N	L	X	U	U	M	V	J	N
U	X	E	E	W	Y	A	R	H	U	R	F	S	M	Y
X	L	I	F	G	F	R	V	P	R	M	Q	N	O	Z
Q	E	E	R	E	U	T	R	I	V	A	Y	D	Z	C
R	M	I	H	J	B	C	P	T	C	Q	M	C	L	O

WORDS IN CONTEXT

Fill in the blanks with words from each box.

principles	pressure	promote	square	guarantees

1. The company _____ that this skin cream will make you look years younger.
2. Students often feel a lot of _____ right before an important exam.
3. There is a statue of the president in the middle of the town _____.
4. When you study the _____ of art, you learn what makes a good painting.
5. Companies often hire celebrities to _____ their products.

self-proclaimed	target	cosmetic	run	dye

6. The company plans to _____ young people. It wants teenagers to buy its products.
7. Martha is a _____ beauty expert, but no one believes it.
8. My parents _____ this company. It's a family business.
9. I buy a lot of _____ products. I like to look beautiful.
10. I don't like the color of my hair. I think I'll _____ it.

market	plain	essential	sags	financial

11. If you want to get a good job, it's _____ to get a good education first.

12. Even though Barbara is _____, she has a lot of friends. Beauty isn't everything.

13. My _____ situation is fine. I have plenty of money.

14. The seat of that chair _____ because it is so old.

15. Most companies _____ their products on TV and in magazines.

WORD FAMILIES
Fill in the blanks with words from each box.

inappropriate (*adjective*) appropriate (*adjective*) appropriately (*adverb*)

1. It is important to dress _____ when you go to a job interview.

2. Putting your feet on the desk is _____ behavior in a classroom.

reluctance (*noun*) reluctant (*adjective*) reluctantly (*adverb*)

3. Because of his shyness, Joe was _____ to invite Myra to the dance.

4. Clara walked _____ to the kitchen and started washing the dishes.

inheritance (*noun*) inheritor (*noun*) inherited (*verb*)

5. After Jiro _____ a lot of money, he took a trip around the world.

6. My grandparents left me a small _____.

SYNONYMS OR ANTONYMS?
Look at the word pairs. Are they synonyms, antonyms, or neither? Check the correct answer.

		Synonyms	Antonyms	Neither
1. everlasting	temporary	☐	☐	☐
2. financial	emotional	☐	☐	☐
3. genuine	artificial	☐	☐	☐
4. quest	search	☐	☐	☐
5. grade	rate	☐	☐	☐
6. elect	choose	☐	☐	☐
7. tattoo	jewelry	☐	☐	☐
8. dye	color	☐	☐	☐
9. essential	unimportant	☐	☐	☐
10. feminine	masculine	☐	☐	☐

SENTENCE COMPLETION
Complete the article with words from the box.

fantasies	tattoos	glamorous	plain	transformation

_____ have become very fashionable. Many young people are walking around with art on their skin. Why do they do it? Most say that they were tired of looking _____ and ordinary. They wanted an exciting life. Did following this fashion give them the _____ life they hoped for? A few people say, "Yes!" They have experienced a _____ and their lives are very different now from what they were before. Their _____ of a new life have become real. Most people, however, say that the fashion is fun, but nothing has really changed in their lives.

WHAT ABOUT YOU?
Speaking
Ask your partner these questions.

1. What cosmetic products do you like to use?

2. What are appropriate clothes to wear in school?

3. What are essential things to bring to school?

4. Would you ever dye your hair? Why or why not?

5. Would you like to get a tattoo? Why or why not?

Writing
Now write about your partner. Use your partner's answers to the questions.
Example: _Bob doesn't use any cosmetic products._

1. _____

2. _____

3. _____

4. _____

5. _____

READING QUIZ

Read the passage and answer the questions. Circle your answers.

Teen Forum/Message Board

Date: March 27
Topic: What does beauty mean to you?

Author	Message
Quest4life	In my opinion, you don't inherit beauty from your parents. Beauty is a virtue that you have to search for on your own. Anyone can wear cosmetics and look glamorous on the outside. To find inner beauty, one must go on a quest, making personal transformations along the way.
Glamorgal	The standards of beauty seem to change every day. Today a woman with a tattoo is beautiful. Tomorrow a tattoo is too masculine and she's having it removed. There is too much pressure to be beautiful in our society. Instead of marketing beautiful bodies, magazines should promote healthy living.
Young@heart	To me, beauty is an everlasting thing. It doesn't matter if your skin sags or your hair turns gray. While some people are reluctant to show their true age, I think genuine people are the most beautiful.
$$$hungry	The most beautiful thing in the world is financial freedom. Money can buy a product that guarantees to make you look younger or more feminine. My goal is to be rich first and beautiful second. If you have money, the world will be a more bearable place.

(line numbers: 5, 10, 15)

MAIN IDEA

1. What are these messages about?

A. Advertisements for beauty products

B. Young people's opinions about beauty

C. Advice from professional beauty experts

D. Reviews of beauty magazines for teenagers

DETAIL

2. What opinion does Quest4life express?

A. Money makes you beautiful.

B. You lose beauty as you age.

C. Everyone should use cosmetics.

D. We must search for inner beauty.

3. Who believes that beauty lasts forever?

A. Quest4life

B. Glamorgal

C. Young@heart

D. $$$hungry

INFERENCE

4. What does Glamorgal believe?

A. Tattoos are unattractive.

B. Health is more important than beauty.

C. It's important to read beauty magazines.

D. Glamorous people have better lives.

VOCABULARY

5. What does *sags* in line 9 mean?

A. Hangs down

B. Looks dirty

C. Turns red

D. Gets wrinkled

6. What does *transformations* in line 4 mean?

A. Goals

B. Friends

C. Changes

D. Decisions

UNIT 5 FANTASY

PEOPLE

PREPARE TO READ
Discuss these questions.

1. What are some methods people use to fly?

2. How could someone fly using the chair in the picture?

WORD FOCUS
Match the words with their definitions.

A.
1. aluminum __   **a.** go up; rise
2. ascend __   **b.** force someone to pay money as a punishment
3. authorities __   **c.** a type of gas that is lighter than air
4. fine __   **d.** people in power
5. helium __   **e.** a type of light metal

B.
1. parachute __   **a.** rules
2. regulations __   **b.** not follow a rule or law
3. shiver __   **c.** twist; tie up
4. tangle __   **d.** shake because of fear or cold
5. violate __   **e.** something used to slow your fall when
                            jumping from a plane

SCAN
A. Guess the answer. Circle *a* or *b*.
Larry Walters used _____ to make a garden chair fly.

a. a small engine   *b.* some balloons

B. Scan the passage quickly to check your answer.

Larry Walters

For most people, a chair is a place to sit and relax. For truck driver Larry Walters, a chair was a way to fly.

From the time he was small, Larry was
5 fascinated by balloons and fantasized about using them to fly. When he was 33 years old, he decided to make his dream come true. He purchased the essential gear—an ordinary **aluminum** garden chair and 42 weather
10 balloons. He also got an air gun because he planned to shoot the balloons when he was ready to land. His girlfriend convinced him to get a **parachute**, too, just in case.

Larry planned to fly 483 kilometers across the
15 Mojave Desert, beginning from the backyard of his girlfriend's house near Los Angeles. On the day of his trip, he tied the chair down with ropes and attached the **helium**-filled balloons to it. Then, he sat down in the chair with his
20 gun and his parachute. He was ready to go.

Larry's friends untied one rope. Suddenly, the other rope broke, and Larry and his chair rose rapidly toward the sky. He **ascended** much more quickly and much higher than he
25 had expected. Before he knew it, he was 5,000 meters above the ground.

Larry's trip wasn't turning out the way he had planned. He was high up in the sky where the air was thin and cold. An airplane
30 pilot spotted him and reported him to the **authorities**. Meanwhile, **shivering** with cold, Larry decided that he wanted to descend, but there was nothing he could do. He had dropped the gun during his ascent. All he could
35 do was float wherever the wind took him.

Eventually, Larry and his chair floated down. The ropes holding the balloons became **tangled** in some power lines, and the chair hung just two meters above the
40 ground. Larry was able to climb down unhurt, but the tangled ropes caused a twenty-minute power blackout in the neighborhood.

Even though the authorities **fined** Larry for **violating** flying **regulations**, he had fulfilled
45 his dream of flying with balloons.

WHICH MEANING?
What does *power* mean in line 38?
1 (*noun*) electricity
2 (*noun*) strength
3 (*noun*) ability

CHECK YOUR COMPREHENSION

Read the passage again and answer the questions. Circle your answers.

MAIN IDEA
1. What is this passage mainly about?
   A. How to make a flying machine
   B. Different ways to travel across the desert
   C. An unusual trip across the desert
   D. A power blackout

DETAIL
2. What was Larry Walters' job?
   A. Pilot
   B. Gardener
   C. Truck driver
   D. Aluminum chair salesman

3. What did Larry take with him on his flying trip?
   A. A gun and a parachute
   B. Drinking water
   C. A warm jacket
   D. Some sandwiches

4. How high in the air did Larry ascend?
   A. 300 meters
   B. 483 meters
   C. 500 meters
   D. 5,000 meters

INFERENCE
5. What did Larry do when he wanted to return to the ground?
   A. He shot the balloons.
   B. He untied the ropes.
   C. He asked a pilot for help.
   D. He waited for the chair to land by itself.

TEXT REFERENCE
6. Which paragraph mentions Larry's reason for making this trip?
   A. The first paragraph
   B. The second paragraph
   C. The third paragraph
   D. The fourth paragraph

PLACES

PREPARE TO READ
Discuss these questions.

1. Would you like to live in the place in the photo? Why or why not?

2. Describe your ideal place to live.

WORD FOCUS
Match the words with their definitions.

A.

1. explore __   **a.** agreement

2. fulfill __   **b.** a gift

3. harmony __   **c.** travel to new places for the first time

4. offering __   **d.** heaven

5. paradise __   **e.** satisfy; complete

B.

1. precious __   **a.** an area

2. region __   **b.** an ideal place

3. starvation __   **c.** valuable

4. unique __   **d.** extreme hunger

5. utopia __   **e.** unlike anything else

SCAN
A. Guess the answer. Circle *a* or *b*.

When did Spaniards explore the Americas?

a. In the 1500s   *b.* In the 1800s

B. Scan the passage quickly to check your answer.

The Search for Utopia

A **unique** place is hidden in a remote area of the Himalayan mountains. People live there in peace and **harmony**, surrounded by the spectacular scenery of snowy mountain peaks,
5 sparkling rivers, and <u>rich</u>, green valleys. This **utopia** is known as *Shangri-La*, a word that in the local language means land of peace or **paradise**.

How can you get to Shangri-La? People
10 have been searching for it for years. It was first mentioned in the novel *Lost Horizon*, written by James Hilton in 1933. Although *Lost Horizon* is a work of fiction, it has inspired many people to search for a real Shangri-La
15 somewhere in the Himalayas. Many believe that if they can just reach this place, they will be able to live a life of peace, harmony, and beauty.

The legend of Shangri-La is not the only
20 story to inspire people to search for a better place. In the 1500s, Spaniards **exploring** the Americas were inspired by the legend of El Dorado to search for a land of gold. Local people told the Spanish explorers of a leader
25 who lived in a city of gold. He celebrated festivals by covering his body with gold dust, and he threw gold and **precious** stones into a lake as **offerings**.

Spanish explorers spent a great deal of time
30 and money in their quest for El Dorado, the land of gold. They ascended high mountains and descended to dangerous, unknown **regions** of the South American jungle. They experienced illness, **starvation**, and death,
35 but they never found El Dorado.

Spanish explorer Ponce de Leon was inspired by another legend—the fountain of youth. He had heard stories of a land filled with beautiful flowers and fruit, friendly people, with gold
40 everywhere and, most importantly, a special river. Anyone who bathed in this river or drank the water would have everlasting youth. Ponce de Leon traveled around Florida and nearby areas tasting the water wherever he went,
45 but he died before he ever discovered the legendary fountain of youth.

In all times and places, people have been inspired to seek a better place where dreams will be **fulfilled**.

WHICH MEANING?
What does *rich* mean in line 5?
1 (*adjective*) heavy but delicious
2 (*adjective*) having a lot of money
3 (*adjective*) full of plant life

CHECK YOUR COMPREHENSION

Read the passage again and answer the questions. Circle your answers.

MAIN IDEA

1. What is this passage mainly about?
   A. Exploring mountains
   B. Good places for vacations
   C. The history of South America
   D. The search for a better place

DETAIL

2. Shangri-La is an imaginary place in
   A. South America
   B. The Himalayas
   C. Florida
   D. Spain

3. Who was James Hilton?
   A. A novelist
   B. A Spanish explorer
   C. A mountain climber
   D. A person who lived in Florida

4. What did Spanish explorers want to find?
   A. A land of peace and harmony
   B. A paradise in the mountains
   C. A lake to bathe in
   D. A city of gold

INFERENCE

5. What did Ponce de Leon want?
   A. A peaceful life
   B. A lot of wealth
   C. Permanent youth
   D. Some land in Florida

TEXT REFERENCE

6. Which paragraph describes the search for El Dorado?
   A. The first paragraph
   B. The second paragraph
   C. The third paragraph
   D. The fourth paragraph

THINGS

PREPARE TO READ
Discuss these questions.

1. What is going on in this photo? Would you like to be there? Why or why not?

2. Where would you go and what would you do on a dream vacation?

WORD FOCUS
Match the words with their definitions.

A.
1. aristocrat __	**a.** a formal dance party
2. astronaut __	**b.** brave; adventurous
3. ball __	**c.** a person of a high social position
4. bold __	**d.** a space traveler
5. elegant __	**e.** beautiful and stylish

B.
1. escort __	**a.** connected to kings and queens
2. finery __	**b.** move at a high speed
3. racetrack __	**c.** beautiful clothes
4. royal __	**d.** a place for car races
5. zoom __	**e.** a person who accompanies you at a social occasion

SCAN
A. Guess the answer. Circle *a* or *b*.

How much did a businessman pay to travel in space?

a. Two million dollars   *b.* Twenty million dollars

B. Scan the passage quickly to check your answer.

Fantasy Vacations

Do you dream about living the glamorous life of royalty? Do you fantasize about the adventure of exploring outer space or the thrill of winning a car race? You can make
5 dreams like these come true. Many people have done it already. In fact, fantasy vacations are becoming more and more popular all around the world.

Is your dream to dance all night at a **royal**
10 **ball**? **Elegant** balls are held in Vienna, Austria every year, and several tourist agencies offer clients the opportunity to attend them. The agencies help their clients select elegant ball <u>dresses</u>, jewelry, and tiaras, so that they can
15 arrive at the balls looking like princesses. The agencies also hire handsome **escorts**. Dressed in their **finery**, these fantasy princesses dance the night away at balls attended by European **aristocrats**, just like real princesses.

20 Maybe your fantasy is to travel in outer space. You don't have to be an **astronaut** to do this, though you probably do have to be a millionaire. Dennis Tito, a businessman from California, was the first tourist in space. His
25 boyhood dream of traveling to space finally came true in 2001, when he was 60 years old. He paid the Russian space program about $20,000,000 to fly him to the International Space Station, where he spent six days. He
30 was soon followed by South African Mark Shuttleworth, who paid a similar amount of money for a trip in 2002.

Perhaps you have a more down-to-earth fantasy, like becoming a race car driver. Many
35 companies offer people the opportunity to spend a day **zooming** around a **racetrack** in a genuine race car. You can spend an afternoon or an entire day driving on a racetrack at speeds of 300 kilometers per hour or more.
40 The less **bold** can choose to ride as a passenger in a car with a professional driver. Either way, you get to experience the thrill of a high-speed ride.

Whatever your fantasy may be, someone
45 can make it come true for you. How much would your dream cost?

WHICH MEANING?
What does *dresses* mean in line 14?
1 (*verb*) decorates
2 (*noun*) items of clothing
3 (*verb*) puts on clothes

CHECK YOUR COMPREHENSION

Read the passage again and answer the questions. Circle your answers.

MAIN IDEA
1. What is this passage mainly about?
  A. Living like royalty
  B. Traveling in outer space
  C. Making dreams come true
  D. Vacationing with millionaires

DETAIL
2. Where can tourists attend royal balls?
  A. Russia
  B. Austria
  C. California
  D. South Africa

3. Who is Dennis Tito?
  A. A businessman from California
  B. The first tourist in space
  C. A millionaire
  D. All of the above

4. How fast can the race cars mentioned in the passage go?
  A. 30 kilometers an hour
  B. 200 kilometers an hour
  C. 300 kilometers an hour
  D. 900 kilometers an hour

INFERENCE
5. What is true about fantasy vacations?
  A. They are a thing of the past.
  B. They are only for millionaires.
  C. They are attractive to many kinds of people.
  D. They are popular mainly in European countries.

TEXT REFERENCE
6. In line 5, *Many people have done it already*, what does the word *it* refer to?
  A. Exploring outer space
  B. Winning a car race
  C. Making a dream come true
  D. Meeting royalty

VOCABULARY REVIEW

CROSSWORD PUZZLE
Complete the crossword using the clues.

Across

1. a rich and perhaps royal person

4. heaven

6. tied up like messy hair or rope

7. an ideal place

8. valuable and often rare

9. beautiful and stylish

Down

1. a person who travels to space

2. rules

3. shake as a result of being cold or scared

5. dying because there is no food

WORDS IN CONTEXT
Fill in the blanks with words from each box.

ascended	zoomed	power	rich	harmony

1. A big tree fell on the electric wires so we lost _____ for several days.

2. Pat _____ past us on his bicycle as we were walking down the road.

3. We live in _____ with our neighbors. We almost never fight.

4. He's an excellent mountain climber. He has _____ Mt. Everest twice.

5. The earth in this valley is very _____; all kinds of plants grow here.

finery	offering	aluminum	authorities	helium

6. In El Dorado, a man threw gold into the lake as an _____.

7. The princess entered the room dressed in all her _____.

8. This chair is made of _____. It's light, but strong.

9. We filled the balloons with _____, then let them float away with the wind.

10. The airport _____ don't allow passengers to enter this area.

parachute	precious	tangled	region	fulfilled

11. I tried to fly a kite, but it became _____ in some tree branches.

12. This _____ of the country becomes very cold in the winter.

13. I like all _____ stones, but diamonds are my favorite.

14. Jane danced with a real prince. That _____ her dream of meeting royalty.

15. A pilot has to know how to use a _____ in case there's an accident with the plane.

WORD FAMILIES
Fill in the blanks with words from each box.

boldness (*noun*)	**bold** (*adjective*)	**boldly** (*adverb*)

1. I think anyone who travels in space is very _____.

2. Ji-young walked _____ to the front of the class and began his speech.

royalty (*noun*)	**royal** (*adjective*)	**royally** (*adverb*)

3. Cynthia moved _____ down the stairs. She looked like a queen.

4. When the prince got married, _____ from all over the world attended his wedding.

violation (*noun*)	**violators** (*noun*)	**violate** (*verb*)

5. _____ of these rules will be fined $100.

6. If you _____ the rules, you will be punished.

WRONG WORD
One word in each group does not fit. Circle the word.

1. rule	regulation	law	story
2. racetrack	garage	highway	road
3. unique	unusual	common	rare
4. steel	gold	plastic	aluminum
5. ball	dance	work	party
6. remain	travel	explore	discover
7. escort	boss	companion	date
8. punishment	reward	fine	penalty
9. region	paradise	utopia	heaven
10. hairstyle	dress	gloves	necktie

SENTENCE COMPLETION
Complete the notice with words from the box.

violates   racetrack   fined   escort   regulations

Springfield Speedway
Information for Visitors

Visitors may drive on the _____ on Saturday and Sunday mornings. Please pay your fee to the manager. You may use your own car or rent a race car.

If this is your first time driving a race car, you must drive with an experienced _____. You cannot drive alone.

Please read the Speedway _____ before driving. These rules are for everybody's safety. Anyone who _____ our rules will be asked to leave the Speedway and may also be _____. Respect your fellow drivers, drive carefully, and have fun.

WHAT ABOUT YOU?
Speaking
Ask your partner these questions.

1. When do you wear elegant clothes?

2. What places would you like to explore?

3. Would you rather go to a racetrack or a ball? Why?

4. What is something precious that you own?

5. Would you like to be an astronaut? Why or why not?

Writing
Now write about your partner. Use your partner's answers to the questions.

Example: <u>Eliza wears elegant clothes when she attends a wedding.</u>

1. _____

2. _____

3. _____

4. _____

5. _____

Read the passage and answer the questions. Circle your answers.

Live Like Cinderella

"May I have this dance, Cinderella?"

Are the daily pressures at work and at home making you tired? Every hard-working woman deserves a break. If you
5 fantasize about living the luxurious life of royalty or of spending your days like a princess with nothing to do all day but look elegant, we at Dream Vacations can help you fulfill your dreams.

10 Our Cinderella Dream vacation package includes:

❀ Four days and five nights at a first-class Vienna, Austria hotel

❀ Three evenings dancing at Vienna's
15 most elegant balls with European aristocrats

❀ An escort for each ball

❀ Transportation to Vienna's finest department stores to purchase
20 finery for the balls

Do you like to explore? For an extra fee, we will include a one-day guided tour of Vienna and the surrounding region. The tour includes visits to Vienna's
25 delightful palaces, where the Austrian royal family once lived.

Be bold. Take advantage of this unique opportunity to live your fantasy. Call Dream Vacations today.

30 *Please note: For current prices, call your local Dream Vacations representative. Vacation packages do not include airfare or meals. Prices subject to change without notice.*

MAIN IDEA

1. Who would be interested in taking the advertised vacation?

A. European aristocrats
B. Women with a dream
C. Businessmen
D. Families

DETAIL

2. How many nights will participants spend in Vienna?

A. Two
B. Three
C. Four
D. Five

3. What is not included in the price of the vacation?

A. Meals
B. Hotel room
C. Shopping trip
D. Escorts

INFERENCE

4. What is the main purpose of taking this vacation?

A. To attend balls
B. To go shopping
C. To tour Vienna
D. To visit palaces

VOCABULARY

5. What does *finery* in line 20 mean?

A. Souvenirs
B. Tickets
C. Clothes
D. Money

6. What does *region* in line 23 mean?

A. Area
B. Roads
C. Stores
D. River

REPTILES

PEOPLE

PREPARE TO READ
Discuss these questions.

1. How can snakes be dangerous? In what ways are they useful?

2. What kinds of jobs involve working with snakes?

WORD FOCUS
Match the words with their definitions.

A.
1. blame __   **a.** a type of poisonous snake
2. carry on __   **b.** give to others in need
3. cobra __   **c.** accuse
4. donate __   **d.** an achievement
5. feat __   **e.** continue

B.
1. lifespan __   **a.** finish your career
2. major __   **b.** important
3. perish __   **c.** the length of time one lives
4. pursue __   **d.** die
5. retire __   **e.** be involved with (a career or hobby)

SCAN
A. Guess the answer. Circle *a* or *b*.
How many days did a man spend in a pen filled with snakes?

a. Three   *b.* Seven

B. Scan the passage quickly to check your answer.

Snake Lovers

Around the world there are men and women who make their living in unusual ways. Most of us would not do such jobs for a day, let alone **pursue** them as a lifelong career.
5 However, the **lifespan** of these people may not be that long. They spend their days working with snakes.

Boonreung Bauchan is listed in the book of *Guinness World Records* for his **feat** of spending
10 seven days in a pen filled with snakes. This Thai snake charmer performed with his pet snakes to earn money to support his family. During his performances, he danced with snakes, held them around his body, and even
15 kissed them. One day, a **cobra** kissed him back. He **perished** before he reached the hospital. Although he left behind several boxes of pet snakes, no one in his family was bold enough to touch them. Instead of
20 **carrying on** with the snake <u>shows</u>, they decided to **donate** the snakes to the zoo.

In Australia, John Cann carries on his family's tradition of reptile shows. His parents started their snake circus in 1919. Cann's mother was
25 called Cleopatra after the queen of Egypt

who was lethally bitten by a snake. Both parents survived their profession and **retired** in good health. Their son has made good use of his lifelong experience with snakes. He now advises
30 the Australia Museum on reptiles and has written several books on snakes and turtles. His goal is not only to entertain, but also to educate his audience on the value of these reptiles and their important role in the environment.

35 In India, Romulus Whitaker doesn't charm snakes or entertain his audience, but he is an active educator and environmentalist. He caught his first snake when he was just three. Now he is the director of the Madras
40 Crocodile Bank and advises **major** international organizations on protecting the habitat of reptiles. Whitaker may be in need of protection himself. He has been bitten three times, but he doesn't **blame** the snakes. He says he's
45 more afraid of people than of snakes.

WHICH MEANING?
What does *shows* mean in line 20?

1 (*verb*) explains
2 (*noun*) performances
3 (*verb*) presents

CHECK YOUR COMPREHENSION

Read the passage again and answer the questions. Circle your answers.

MAIN IDEA
1. What is this passage mainly about?
   A. Snake shows
   B. The dangers of snakes
   C. Snakes in different countries
   D. Working with snakes and other reptiles

DETAIL
2. What happened after Boonreung Bauchan died from a cobra bite?
   A. The cobra was killed.
   B. People bought his pet snakes.
   C. His family gave his snakes away.
   D. His family continued giving snake shows.

3. What did John Cann's parents do?
   A. They wrote a book about snakes and turtles.
   B. They gave a museum advice about reptiles.
   C. They performed in reptile shows.
   D. They opened a pet store.

4. Who is Romulus Whitaker?
   A. An entertainer
   B. A snake charmer
   C. A crocodile trainer
   D. An environmentalist

INFERENCE
5. What is probably true about Boonreung Bauchan's family?
   A. They enjoy playing with snakes.
   B. They are environmentalists.
   C. They are not wealthy.
   D. They like cobras.

TEXT REFERENCE
6. In line 26, *who was lethally bitten by a snake*, what does the word *who* refer to?
   A. The queen of Egypt
   B. John Cann
   C. John Cann's mother
   D. Cleopatra's son

PLACES

a Komodo dragon

PREPARE TO READ
Discuss these questions.

1. Look at the Komodo dragon in the photo. How large do you think it is?

2. What do you think a Komodo dragon eats?

WORD FOCUS
Match the words with their definitions.

A.

1. bacteria __   **a.** eat
2. cautious __   **b.** the smallest living things—many cause diseases
3. claw __   **c.** careful
4. consume __   **d.** move quickly
5. dart __   **e.** a sharp part of an animal's foot

B.

1. forked __   **a.** a type of reptile
2. keep away __   **b.** walk slowly and heavily
3. lizard __   **c.** divided at one end
4. plod __   **d.** not aware
5. unsuspecting __   **e.** stay at a distance

SCAN
A. Guess the answer. Circle *a* or *b*.

Where do Komodo dragons live?

a. Indonesia   *b.* India

B. Scan the passage quickly to check your answer.

Komodo National Park and Its Dragons

If you want to see Komodo dragons, Komodo National Park in Indonesia is the place to go. The park is located on Komodo and other nearby islands. This remote region is the only
5 place in the world where Komodo dragons live. They can be found all over the park, from the pink sandy beaches to the hills and rocky mountains.

A Komodo dragon is a predator. It **plods**
10 through the jungle in pursuit of a meal, swinging its head from side to side and **darting** its **forked** tongue in and out of its mouth. When a deer appears, the dragon hides in the grass. Then, the dragon rushes out and attacks
15 the **unsuspecting** animal with its sharp teeth and **claws**. The dragon opens its jaws wide and **consumes** almost the entire deer. It won't need to have another meal for weeks.

Even if a deer escapes a dragon attack, it
20 will perish within a few days. This is because a dragon carries lethal **bacteria** in its mouth. The bacteria kill any animal the dragon bites. With its sharp sense of smell, the dragon can soon find the injured deer and enjoy its meal.
25 After eating a meal, a large dragon might

weigh as much as 250 kilos. They usually weigh about half that amount. The largest male dragons are up to three meters long. Females are usually a little over two meters
30 long and weigh about 65 kilos. Komodo dragons are the largest **lizards** in the world.

Baby dragons, of course, are much smaller. They live in trees and eat birds' eggs, insects, and small animals. As they <u>grow</u>, they eat
35 birds, rats, and mice. When they are about four or five years old and one meter long, they are too large to climb trees. Then, they start living on the ground like adults.

Adult dragons usually eat deer, but they eat
40 other animals as well. They might eat snakes, birds, fish, wild pigs, and even smaller dragons. That's why baby dragons **keep away** from their parents. Everybody has to be **cautious** when a large Komodo dragon is nearby,
45 including tourists who visit the park.

WHICH MEANING?
What does *grow* mean in line 34?
1 (*verb*) increase
2 (*verb*) take care of plants
3 (*verb*) become bigger

CHECK YOUR COMPREHENSION

Read the passage again and answer the questions. Circle your answers.

MAIN IDEA
1. What is this passage mainly about?
A. Predators
B. Different kinds of lizards
C. A place with an unusual animal
D. An island with beautiful beaches

DETAIL
2. What does a Komodo dragon do before it attacks a deer?
A. It hides in the grass.
B. It climbs a tree.
C. It waits behind a rock.
D. It stands on the beach.

3. What does a Komodo dragon use to kill a deer?
A. Teeth
B. Claws
C. Bacteria
D. All of the above

4. How long are the largest Komodo dragons?
A. One meter
B. A little over two meters
C. Close to three meters
D. Six and a half meters

INFERENCE
5. After eating a deer, why doesn't a Komodo dragon eat again for several weeks?
A. Because it's too tired
B. Because it just ate a huge meal
C. Because it's very difficult to kill a deer
D. Because it takes a long time to find another deer

TEXT ORGANIZATION
6. Which paragraph describes the habits of baby Komodo dragons?
A. The third paragraph
B. The fourth paragraph
C. The fifth paragraph
D. The sixth paragraph

THINGS

turtles

PREPARE TO READ
Discuss these questions.

1. Name some reptiles. Which ones live in your country?

2. Would you enjoy walking in the woods and looking for little animals? Why or why not?

WORD FOCUS
Match the words with their definitions.

A.

1. amphibians __   **a.** look closely
2. creep __   **b.** an underground source of metal or precious stones
3. mine __   **c.** having rough skin
4. peer __   **d.** move slowly
5. scaly __   **e.** animals (such as frogs) born in water that can also live on land

B.

1. scan __   **a.** how a snake moves
2. slimy __   **b.** move the eyes quickly over an area
3. slithery __   **c.** an area of wet land
4. swamp __   **d.** smooth and wet
5. thorn __   **e.** something sharp on a branch

SCAN
A. Guess the answer. Circle *a* or *b*.
Herping means

a. reading about reptiles and amphibians.
b. looking for reptiles and amphibians.

B. Scan the passage quickly to check your answer.

TRACK 19 Herping

Two friends take a walk on a pleasant spring day. Although the weather is warm, they wear long pants and gloves. One of them carries a long pole. They cross the fields, their eyes
5 constantly **scanning** the ground. When they find a log or large stone, they lift it up and **peer** into the darkness beneath. You might imagine they are trying to find a buried chest packed with gold or a **mine** filled with precious
10 diamonds. But the treasure they seek is something very different. It is a **slithery** snake, a **slimy** frog, or a **scaly** lizard.

This activity—looking for reptiles and **amphibians** in their native habitat—is called
15 *herping*. This name comes from a word which means **creeping**. Herpers may push their way through **thorn** bushes, ascend rocky hillsides, or plod through wet **swamps** in pursuit of slimy, scaly, creeping creatures. The reward is
20 discovering a fat snake warming itself on a sunny rock, or observing a turtle hunting <u>flies</u> in a remote pond.

In addition to a sense of adventure and some knowledge of the habits of slimy and
25 scaly creatures, just a few basic items of equipment are required for herping. Many herpers carry a snake stick—a long pole with a type of hook on the end. It's useful for picking up snakes as well as for lifting logs and stones.
30 A flashlight is good for finding animals hiding in dark places or for herping at night. Most herpers also take cameras and notebooks with them so they can record their discoveries. They might wear long pants and gloves for
35 protection while walking through thorn bushes or picking up stones and logs. Thick boots protect herpers from snakebites. And, just in case their boots aren't thick enough, smart herpers also carry a kit for
40 treating snakebites.

Herping can be done anywhere. A herper might start in his or her own backyard or travel to far away jungles and deserts in quest of rare species. Reptiles and amphibians can be found
45 all over the world, and so can herpers.

WHICH MEANING?
What does *flies* mean in line 21?

1 (*verb*) escapes
2 (*verb*) travels in the air
3 (*noun*) certain flying insects

CHECK YOUR COMPREHENSION

Read the passage again and answer the questions. Circle your answers.

MAIN IDEA
1. What is this passage mainly about?
   A. Snakebites
   B. Animal photography
   C. A surprising hobby
   D. Reptiles of the world

DETAIL
2. What is the meaning of the word that *herping* comes from?
   A. Slimy
   B. Scaly
   C. Creeping
   D. Wet

3. Why do herpers carry poles?
   A. To pick up snakes
   B. To walk more easily
   C. To kill poisonous animals
   D. To dig holes in the ground

4. How do herpers protect themselves from snakebites?
   A. By wearing long pants
   B. By carrying a flashlight
   C. By wearing thick boots
   D. By looking carefully under rocks

INFERENCE
5. Which of the following would be the least interesting to a herper?
   A. A toad sitting in a garden
   B. A snake resting in the woods
   C. A lizard climbing a tree in a park
   D. A turtle catching flies in a cage in the zoo

TEXT ORGANIZATION
6. Which paragraph describes a typical herping trip?
   A. The first paragraph
   B. The second paragraph
   C. The third paragraph
   D. The fourth paragraph

VOCABULARY REVIEW

SCRAMBLED WORDS
Unscramble the words to complete the sentences.

1. Some frogs are so _____ that they slither out of your hands when you grab them. (**mlsiy**)

2. Many amphibians live in _____ where it's warm and wet. (**mwsaps**)

3. Lizards catch _____ insects with their long tongues. (**uussnpceitng**)

4. Young herpetologists are taught to be _____ near cobras. (**tacuuios**)

5. Even spending an hour in a pen with snakes is a major _____. (**tefa**)

6. The Komodo dragon _____ through the jungle, pursuing its next meal. (**lpsod**)

7. The lizard tasted the air with its _____ tongue. (**kdorfe**)

8. The child who found the snake egg _____ it to the zoo. (**dodaten**)

9. Though he _____ from giving reptile shows, he continued herping. (**ereirtd**)

10. The snake charmer _____ into the box to see if the cobra was still sleeping. (**eerepd**)

WORDS IN CONTEXT
Fill in the blanks with words from each box.

perish	blame	major	pursue	lifespan

1. After a Komodo dragon attacks a deer, the deer will _____ quickly.

2. Some insects live only a few weeks. They have a very short _____.

3. You can't _____ the snake for biting you. That's just its natural behavior.

4. If you are interested in wild animals, you could _____ a career at a zoo.

5. Komodo dragons are the _____ attraction at Komodo National Park.

show	darted	scanned	consumed	slithery

6. The Komodo dragon _____ the jungle, looking for a deer.

7. I saw a funny _____ on TV last night. It really made me laugh.

8. Richard was so hungry that he _____ an entire pizza by himself.

9. The _____ snakes moved rapidly across the ground.

10. The cat _____ across the room. We couldn't catch it.

crept	grow	flies	claws	slimy

11. Baby birds _____ quickly. After a few weeks, they are ready to leave the nest.

12. The frog sat at the edge of the pond, looking for _____ to eat.

13. I don't like to touch frogs because they feel so _____.

14. The turtle _____ quietly through the woods, looking for water.

15. Most lizards have sharp _____. They can use them to dig holes.

WORD FAMILIES

Fill in the blanks with words from each box.

mines (*noun*)	**miner** (*noun*)	**mining** (*noun*)

1. The work of a _____ is very difficult and dangerous.

2. There are many diamond _____ in Africa.

caution (*noun*)	**cautious** (*adjective*)	**cautiously** (*adverb*)

3. There is a lot of traffic here. Be _____ when you cross the street.

4. He picked up the snake very _____.

donation (*noun*)	**donor** (*noun*)	**donated** (*verb*)

5. The Jones family _____ several pieces of art to the museum.

6. Their _____ made the museum director very happy.

TRUE OR FALSE?

Are the following sentences true or false? Circle your answers.

1. A Komodo dragon has a forked tongue. TRUE FALSE

2. Lizards have scaly skin. TRUE FALSE

3. A swamp is usually dry. TRUE FALSE

4. Snakes have sharp claws. TRUE FALSE

5. Adult Komodo dragons eat flies. TRUE FALSE

6. A cobra makes a good pet for a child. TRUE FALSE

7. A herper's skin is slimy. TRUE FALSE

8. Roses have thorns. TRUE FALSE

9. A frog is an example of an amphibian. TRUE FALSE

10. Bacteria can cause diseases. TRUE FALSE

PHRASAL VERBS
Circle the correct words.

1. When George goes herping, he usually *carries / carries on* a camera and a notebook.

2. He *carried / carried on* with his snake show even though a cobra killed his partner.

3. I am afraid of lizards so I usually try to *keep / keep away* from them.

4. My brother *keeps / keeps away* his pet lizard in a large cage in the living room.

5. Bill wants to lose weight so he has to *keep / keep away* from sweets.

6. You should always *carry / carry on* a snakebite kit when you go herping.

WHAT ABOUT YOU?
Speaking
Ask your partner these questions.

1. What careers are you interested in pursuing?

2. When do you consume a lot of food?

3. What shows do you like on TV?

4. Where have you seen amphibians in the wild?

5. Which animals do you prefer to keep away from?

Writing
Now write about your partner. Use your partner's answers to the questions.

Example: <u>Eun-mi is interested in pursuing a career as an engineer.</u>

1. _____

2. _____

3. _____

4. _____

5. _____

READING QUIZ

Read the passage and answer the questions. Circle your answers.

Making a Home for Your Lizard

Choosing a lizard as a pet is a major decision; the average lifespan of a lizard in captivity is ten to twenty years. Unlike many other pets, lizards are more suitable
5 for observation than handling. It is essential that you review proper cage care before you bring your lizard home.

Here are a few tips:

✘ Your lizard's cage should be made of
10 glass or metal rather than wood. Cages that are difficult to clean lead to higher levels of bacteria and a greater risk of disease.

✘ Like amphibians, reptiles are
15 cold-blooded, which means they do not make their own body heat. You need to provide a heat source for your lizard, which you can do by placing a light bulb at one end of
20 the cage.

✘ Be cautious when choosing the location for your cage. Lizards are not social creatures, and they don't like to watch TV shows. Some have
25 even perished when placed too close to a TV.

✘ Create a comfortable and natural environment for your pet. Make sure the cage is big enough for the lizard
30 to creep around. Also, give your pet places to hide. Most lizards like to hide behind branches or rocks, peering out at unsuspecting prey and consuming food in privacy.

MAIN IDEA

1. What is this passage mainly about?
- **A.** Which lizards make the best pets
- **B.** Arranging a cage for a pet lizard
- **C.** A lizard's natural environment
- **D.** Observing lizards at the zoo

DETAIL

2. What is something that a pet lizard likes to do?
- **A.** Watch TV
- **B.** Play with people
- **C.** Hide behind rocks
- **D.** Turn on a light bulb

INFERENCE

3. What might happen to a lizard living in a wooden cage?
- **A.** It might escape.
- **B.** It might get sick.
- **C.** It might be too cold.
- **D.** It might feel uncomfortable.

TEXT ORGANIZATION

4. Which tip talks about keeping a lizard warm?
- **A.** The first tip
- **B.** The second tip
- **C.** The third tip
- **D.** The fourth tip

VOCABULARY

5. What does *cautious* in line 21 mean?
- **A.** Kind
- **B.** Smart
- **C.** Certain
- **D.** Careful

6. What does *creep* in line 30 mean?
- **A.** Touch
- **B.** Move
- **C.** Look
- **D.** Jump

FORTUNE-TELLING

PEOPLE

Jeanne Dixon

PREPARE TO READ
Discuss these questions.

1. What are some ways people predict the future?

2. Do you know of any famous fortune-tellers? Who are they?

WORD FOCUS
Match the words with their definitions.

A.
1. accurately ___
2. assassination ___
3. astrology ___
4. charity ___
5. earthquake ___

  a. correctly
  b. murder
  c. movement or shaking of the earth
  d. an organization that helps the poor
  e. a system of using the stars to predict the future

B.
1. palm ___
2. predict ___
3. stray ___
4. vegetarian ___
5. vision ___

  a. lost
  b. the inner surface of the hand
  c. a mental picture
  d. guess what will happen in the future
  e. a person who doesn't eat meat

SCAN
A. Guess the answer. Circle *a* or *b*.
In 1964 there was a big earthquake in

a. Alaska.   *b.* London.

B. Scan the passage quickly to check your answer.

Jeanne Dixon

Jeanne Dixon began making predictions when she was a little girl. She had a crystal ball that she used to peer into the future. She correctly **predicted** several events, including the death
5 of her grandfather. She also learned to use **astrology**. When she was just eight years old, a **palm** reader told her fortune. The palm reader said that Jeanne would become famous for her unique ability to predict the future.

10 Dixon made many predictions about the future throughout her life, but the one that brought her the most fame was her prediction of the **assassination** of President Kennedy. In 1952, she had a **vision**. She saw a man with
15 blue eyes living in the White House. He was going to die a violent death. Eight years later, John Kennedy, a man with blue eyes, became president of the United States. On November 22, 1963, Jeanne told her friends, "Something
20 terrible is going to happen today." Then, they heard an announcement. President Kennedy had been shot.

Another of Dixon's major predictions was the death of President Kennedy's brother
25 Robert. One day, she was walking through a hotel in Los Angeles. Suddenly, she stopped and said, "Robert Kennedy is going to be killed here." Soon after that, in June 1968, Robert Kennedy was shot in that <u>exact</u> place.

30 Dixon **accurately** predicted the deaths of several other celebrities. She also predicted other kinds of events, for example, a big **earthquake** in Alaska in 1964. She made a number of inaccurate predictions as well,
35 but people don't seem to remember as many of these.

Dixon didn't keep any fees she earned from making predictions. She donated all the money to a **charity** that supported educational and
40 health projects for children. She was a **vegetarian** and often prepared healthy food for elderly people. She also liked to help animals and took care of many **stray** cats and dogs.

45 Jeanne Dixon died in 1997, but she left behind several predictions which could still come true. One of them is that intelligent life will be discovered on another planet.

WHICH MEANING?
What does *exact* mean in line 29?
1 (*adjective*) specific; precise
2 (*verb*) force to give
3 (*adjective*) careful

CHECK YOUR COMPREHENSION

Read the passage again and answer the questions. Circle your answers.

MAIN IDEA
1. What is this passage mainly about?
  A. Using astrology
  B. A famous palm reader
  C. Assassinations of famous people
  D. A woman who predicted the future

DETAIL
2. What did Jeanne Dixon predict when she was a little girl?
  A. Life on other planets
  B. An earthquake
  C. Stray animals
  D. A death

3. Who predicted Jeanne Dixon's future?
  A. An astrologer
  B. A palm reader
  C. A crystal ball reader
  D. Jeanne's grandfather

4. What happened in 1968?
  A. John Kennedy lived in the White House.
  B. There was an earthquake in Alaska.
  C. President Kennedy's brother was killed.
  D. Jeanne Dixon started a charity for elderly people.

INFERENCE
5. What is true about Jeanne Dixon?
  A. She didn't eat meat.
  B. She didn't like children.
  C. All her predictions were correct.
  D. She became rich from making predictions.

TEXT ORGANIZATION
6. In line 11, *but the one that brought her the most fame*, what does the word *one* refer to?
  A. An assassination
  B. A prediction
  C. A president
  D. A woman

PLACES

PREPARE TO READ
Discuss these questions.

1. Where in your city can you find fortune-tellers?

2. Do you like to visit fortune-tellers? Why or why not?

WORD FOCUS
Match the words with their definitions.

A.
1. architecture __   **a.** something that holds something else
2. container __   **b.** explain the meaning
3. guidance __   **c.** building style
4. incense __   **d.** advice
5. interpret __   **e.** something you burn to produce a pleasant smell

B.
1. intricate __   **a.** ask or wish for something (often religious)
2. noted __   **b.** a small river
3. pray __   **c.** full of details
4. stream __   **d.** a religious building
5. temple __   **e.** known for something

SCAN
A. Guess if this is true or false. Circle *a* or *b*.
Wong Tai Sin Temple is in Hawaii.

a. True   *b.* False

B. Scan the passage quickly to check your answer.

Wong Tai Sin Temple

TRACK 21

Wong Tai Sin Temple, with its colorful **architecture** and peaceful gardens, <u>sits</u> among the high-rise buildings of Hong Kong. It is one of the more popular places
5 to visit in the city. It is especially known for the fortune-tellers that work there.

People visit the **temple** to honor Wong Tai Sin, a shepherd who lived hundreds of years ago. According to legend, at the age of fifteen
10 he learned the secret of making a medicine that could cure all illnesses. He lived alone for forty years while he worked to perfect this magic medicine.

Nowadays, visitors to the temple bring
15 flowers and **incense** as offerings for Wong Tai Sin. They **pray** for good health and for good luck in business. Most of all, they pray for **guidance** for the future. This is because Wong Tai Sin was known not only for his ability to
20 cure illnesses, but also for his skill at correctly predicting the future. The temple has the largest concentration of fortune-tellers in Asia. There can be as many as 150 fortune-tellers working there at any one time.

25 The most common fortune-telling method at the temple is the use of fortune sticks, called *chim*. Each *chim* has a number on it. You shake a **container** of sticks until one falls out. Then, you take the stick to a fortune-
30 teller, who will **interpret** it for you. If you want to try something different, there are other fortune-telling methods to choose from. For a small fee, a fortune-teller will read your face or palm, consult the ancient book, the *I*
35 *Ching*, or use astrology to predict your future.

Wong Tai Sin Temple is **noted** for its brightly colored buildings decorated with beautiful paintings and **intricate** carvings. It also contains the Good Wish Garden with a
40 **stream**, waterfall, and ponds. If you want to know your future, or just want to enjoy a few moments of the present in a beautiful spot, visit Wong Tai Sin Temple.

WHICH MEANING?
What does *sits* mean in line 2?

1 (*verb*) is on a chair
2 (*verb*) models for a painting
3 (*verb*) is in a place

CHECK YOUR COMPREHENSION

Read the passage again and answer the questions. Circle your answers.

MAIN IDEA

1. What is this passage mainly about?
  A. An ancient shepherd
  B. A popular place to visit
  C. Tourist sites in Hong Kong
  D. Chinese fortune-telling methods

DETAIL

2. According to the passage, what happened when Wong Tai Sin was fifteen?
  A. He started a business.
  B. He became a shepherd.
  C. He began telling fortunes.
  D. He learned about a magic medicine.

3. What can you see on each fortune stick?
  A. A name
  B. A picture
  C. A flower
  D. A number

4. What can you see inside Wong Tai Sin Temple?
  A. A sheep
  B. A garden
  C. A large river
  D. A high-rise building

INFERENCE

5. What is probably true about Wong Tai Sin Temple?
  A. It's very modern.
  B. It's rarely crowded.
  C. It's pretty to look at.
  D. It's expensive to enter.

TEXT REFERENCE

6. Which paragraph mentions different fortune-telling methods?
  A. The second paragraph
  B. The third paragraph
  C. The fourth paragraph
  D. The fifth paragraph

THINGS

tea leaves

PREPARE TO READ
Discuss these questions.

1. Can you see any shapes in the tea leaves? What things do those shapes look like?

2. How do you think fortune-tellers use tea leaves to tell the future?

WORD FOCUS
Match the words with their definitions.

A.
1. brew __   **a.** throw away
2. discard __   **b.** having a nice smell
3. drain __   **c.** prepare tea
4. fragrant __   **d.** the part of a cup that you hold
5. handle __   **e.** remove water

B.
1. ladder __   **a.** very hot
2. liquid __   **b.** a small plate under a teacup
3. saucer __   **c.** something used for climbing
4. steaming __   **d.** suddenly
5. unexpectedly __ **e.** water or similar material

SCAN
A. Guess the answer. Circle *a* or *b*.
In the art of reading tea leaves, a bird represents

a. good luck.   *b.* bad luck.

B. Scan the passage quickly to check your answer.

Tea Leaves

The art of predicting the future with tea leaves has been practiced in both Asia and Europe for centuries. It's not hard to try doing it yourself.

5   First, **brew** yourself a cup of tea. You can use any kind of loose tea, but it's best to drink it from a wide, white cup. This makes it easy to see the leaves. Relax and enjoy your tea. Drink it all, but leave a spoonful at the bottom
10 of the cup. Now pick up the cup and move it three times from right to left. Turn it upside down over a **saucer** to let the **liquid drain** out. Turn it right side up again, and now you are ready to read the leaves.

15   When you interpret the leaves, pay attention to their position in the cup. Leaves near the top represent the near future, while leaves near the bottom represent the distant future. Leaves near the cup's **handle** represent
20 yourself or your home. The images in the leaves aren't always distinct, but if you look carefully, some pictures will <u>appear</u>.

    Both birds and airplanes mean that you will make a journey. Birds also represent good
25 luck. A cross or a snake, on the other hand, means that bad luck will come your way. A baby means that you will have small worries. **Ladders** and stars mean that you will reach your dream. Apples mean the same.

30   If you need money, look for a diamond, but be careful of clouds. Diamonds mean that you will receive money **unexpectedly**, but clouds mean that you will have financial problems. If you are looking for love, maybe
35 you will see a moon or a cage in the leaves. A moon represents romance, and a cage represents marriage.

    Both trees and books are lucky symbols. Trees represent good health and long life,
40 and an open book means good news. Eyeglasses mean that good and surprising things will happen.

    Everybody likes to relax with a **steaming** cup of **fragrant** tea, but it can be more than
45 just a delicious drink. After you've enjoyed your tea, don't **discard** the leaves until you've read your future.

WHICH MEANING?
What does *appear* mean in line 22?

1 (*verb*) seem
2 (*verb*) come into view
3 (*verb*) perform

CHECK YOUR COMPREHENSION

Read the passage again and answer the questions. Circle your answers.

MAIN IDEA

1. What is this passage mainly about?
   A. Looking for love
   B. How to have a tea party
   C. Predicting the future in a tea cup
   D. Fortune-telling around the world

DETAIL

2. Which leaves represent your home?
   A. Leaves near the handle of the cup
   B. Leaves near the bottom of the cup
   C. Leaves near the top of the cup
   D. Leaves on the cup's saucer

3. Which image means that you will reach your dreams?
   A. Diamonds
   B. Airplanes
   C. Apples
   D. Babies

4. What does a tree represent?
   A. Good news
   B. Surprises
   C. Long life
   D. Money

INFERENCE

5. What could clouds mean?
   A. Someone in your home has financial worries.
   B. You might lose something in the distant future.
   C. You will have money problems soon.
   D. You will never find love.

TEXT ORGANIZATION

6. Which paragraph explains how to prepare the tea leaves for reading?
   A. The first paragraph
   B. The second paragraph
   C. The third paragraph
   D. The fourth paragraph

VOCABULARY REVIEW

CROSSWORD PUZZLE
Complete the crossword using the clues.

Across

4. shaking of the ground

6. throw away

8. rich in details

9. the study of stars and planets and their effect on people's personalities

10. explain the meaning

Down

1. prepare coffee or tea

2. having a pleasing smell

3. guess what will happen in the future

5. a person who does not eat meat

7. helpful advice

WORDS IN CONTEXT
Fill in the blanks with words from each box.

vision	architecture	incense	temple	stream

1. This _____ gets a lot of visitors. It's a beautiful and peaceful religious place.

2. The fortune-teller had a _____. In her mind she saw an earthquake.

3. There is a _____ running through the garden. We can go fishing there.

4. Tourists visit this city to see the _____. There are a lot of pretty buildings here.

5. People burn _____ to make a room smell nice.

pray	sits	handle	ladder	liquid

6. People visit the temple to _____ for good luck.

7. If we get a _____, we can climb this tree and pick some apples.

8. On a hot day you need to drink plenty of _____.

9. That cup of tea is very hot. Pick it up by the _____.

10. Their house _____ on top of a hill. It's a beautiful location.

appeared	charity	vegetarian	steaming	palm

11. She gave some money to a _____ that helps poor children.

12. It's nice to have a _____ bowl of soup on a cold day.

13. After a cloudy morning, the sun _____ in the sky.

14. The fortune-teller looked at the _____ of my hand and told me my future.

15. Roger refused to eat a hamburger because he's a _____.

WORD FAMILIES

Fill in the blanks with words from each box.

assassination (*noun*)	assassin (*noun*)	assassinated (*verb*)

1. They caught the _____ just a few hours after he killed the emperor.

2. The _____ of the president was a terrible event.

accuracy (*noun*)	accurate (*adjective*)	accurately (*adverb*)

3. He answered all the questions _____.

4. Most of her predictions have been _____.

astrology (*noun*)	astrologer (*noun*)	astrological (*adjective*)

5. She asked an _____ to predict her future.

6. I don't believe in _____ predictions.

SYNONYMS OR ANTONYMS?

Look at the word pairs. Are they synonyms, antonyms, or neither? Check the correct answer.

		Synonyms	Antonyms	Neither
1. palm	finger	☐	☐	☐
2. container	box	☐	☐	☐
3. steaming	freezing	☐	☐	☐
4. stray	lost	☐	☐	☐
5. accurate	wrong	☐	☐	☐
6. noted	unknown	☐	☐	☐
7. drain	water	☐	☐	☐
8. unexpectedly	surprisingly	☐	☐	☐
9. vegetarian	vegetable	☐	☐	☐
10. saucer	plate	☐	☐	☐

SENTENCE COMPLETION
Complete the e-mail with words from the box.

exact   interpreted   predicted   unexpectedly   brewed   stream

To: Bob Brown
From: Shirley Waxman
Subject: My future

Hi Bob,

Guess what? I visited a fortune-teller today. He _____ my future by reading tea leaves. He told me some things that will happen to me. It was really fun. First, he _____ some tea. We drank it, then he _____ the tea leaves. He said he saw a _____ or small river. That means I'll take a trip. I asked him when the trip will be. He said that the leaves don't tell the _____ date, but the trip will be soon. Maybe it means I'll visit you. I hope so! Maybe I'll arrive at your house _____. It'll be a surprise for you.

See you soon (I hope),

Shirley

WHAT ABOUT YOU?
Speaking
Ask your partner these questions.

1. Where does your house sit?

2. What kind of container do you use to hold your pens?

3. When do you use a ladder?

4. Who do you ask for guidance?

5. What kind of architecture do you like?

Writing
Now write about your partner. Use your partner's answers to the questions.
Example: Jin's house sits on a busy street.

1. _____

2. _____

3. _____

4. _____

5. _____

READING QUIZ

Read the passage and answer the questions. Circle your answers.

To: Allison Dubois
From: Mia Roberts
Subject: My visions

Dear Allison Dubois,

I am obsessed with *Medium*, which in my opinion is the only accurate TV show about psychic visions. At first, I didn't realize that the character of Allison Dubois was based on a real person. However, when I heard that in real life you are a psychic who helps
5 the police solve crimes, I knew I had to contact you.

I, too, have visions. I don't communicate with the dead like you, but I have seen crime scenes. For example, I once had a vision of a missing man in a container of liquid, and that same day the police found him in a swimming pool.

Whenever I tell my friends or family that I have visions, they always laugh and ask
10 me to read their palms or to interpret their astrological charts. Nobody takes me seriously. I'm worried that one day I will predict something big like an earthquake or an assassination, and I won't know what to do or who to tell.

I've been praying that my visions would go away, but they are only getting stronger. If you can offer me any guidance, please write to me!

Thank you,

Mia Roberts

MAIN IDEA

1. Why did Mia write this e-mail?

A. To ask for guidance
B. To report a crime
C. To tell Allison about a TV show
D. To offer her fortune-telling services

DETAIL

2. Who is Allison Dubois?

A. A palm reader
B. A close friend of Mia's
C. The director of a TV show
D. A psychic who solves crimes

INFERENCE

3. How does Mia feel about her visions?

A. She's worried about them.
B. She enjoys them.
C. She laughs at them.
D. She's angry about them.

TEXT ORGANIZATION

4. Which paragraph describes one of Mia's visions?

A. The first paragraph
B. The second paragraph
C. The third paragraph
D. The fourth paragraph

VOCABULARY

5. What does *liquid* in line 8 mean?

A. Water
B. Air
C. Sand
D. Food

6. What does *interpret* in line 10 mean?

A. Buy
B. Make
C. Give
D. Explain

DISASTERS

PEOPLE

Ari Afrizal, tsunami survivor

PREPARE TO READ
Discuss these questions.

1. What do you remember about the tsunami of 2004?

2. Can we get advance warning of a tsunami? What can be done to survive one?

WORD FOCUS
Match the words with their definitions.

A.

1. avoid __   **a.** a terrible event
2. colleague __   **b.** float
3. debris __   **c.** a person you work with
4. disaster __   **d.** trash
5. drift __   **e.** prevent

B.

1. inland __   **a.** a very large wave caused by an earthquake
2. leak __   **b.** away from the ocean
3. raft __   **c.** a type of small, flat boat
4. swiftly __   **d.** let water pass through a small hole
5. tsunami __   **e.** quickly

SCAN
A. Guess if this is true or false. Circle *a* or *b*.
On the morning of the 2004 tsunami the weather was stormy.

a. True   *b.* False

B. Scan the passage quickly to check your answer.

TRACK 23 # Ari Afrizal

When Ari Afrizal went to work on December 26, 2004, he had no <u>reason</u> to expect anything unusual. The weather was nice, and everything seemed normal. Unfortunately,
5 it was the day the deadly **tsunami** struck countries all around the Indian Ocean. Even worse, Ari was in the Aceh province of Indonesia, one of the areas hardest hit by the **disaster**.

10   Ari and his **colleagues** were working on the construction of a house when the tsunami struck. When they saw the giant wave approaching unexpectedly, swallowing everything in its way, they dropped their
15 tools and ran as fast as they could toward a nearby hill. The wave caught up with them quickly, pushing them **swiftly inland** before pulling them back out to sea. Ari was separated from his companions and spent the next days
20 **drifting** in the water alone.

   The sea was full of **debris** that the tsunami had grabbed from the land—trees, logs, boats, and pieces of buildings that had all once been part of people's lives. A stray piece

25 of wood drifted by Ari, and he grabbed on to it. He floated like that until the next day when he saw a small boat. It was damaged, but he was able to climb onto it. He stayed there for several days, but the boat was **leaking** badly.
30 He knew that he would have to find something better. Finally, a fishing **raft** came floating by. Although there were no people on the raft, Ari discovered a small container of fresh water and some clothes. He remained on the raft for
35 days and **avoided** starvation by eating coconuts that were floating in the sea.

   Ari waved at several boats that came into his view, but none of them saw him. He began to believe that he would never be
40 rescued. One day, a large ship came by, and Ari waved and whistled at it. This time he was lucky. The ship picked him up and took him safely back to land. Ari had been floating alone at sea for two weeks. No other tsunami
45 survivor had been at sea that long.

WHICH MEANING?
What does *reason* mean in line 2?
  1 (*noun*) intelligence
  2 (*verb*) argue
  3 (*noun*) cause

CHECK YOUR COMPREHENSION

Read the passage again and answer the questions. Circle your answers.

MAIN IDEA
1. What is the main topic of this passage?
  A. Places hit by the tsunami
  B. The cause of the tsunami
  C. Tsunami rescue workers
  D. A tsunami victim

DETAIL
2. What was Ari Afrizal's job?
  A. Fisherman
  B. House builder
  C. Ship's captain
  D. Weatherman

3. What did Ari Afrizal find on the raft that helped him survive?
  A. Fish
  B. Water
  C. Coconuts
  D. All of the above

4. How long was Ari Afrizal at sea before being rescued?
  A. Two hours
  B. Two days
  C. Two weeks
  D. Two months

INFERENCE
5. Why did Ari Afrizal leave the small boat to get on the raft?
  A. The boat was too little.
  B. The boat moved too slowly.
  C. He thought the boat might sink.
  D. There wasn't any food on the boat.

TEXT REFERENCE
6. Which paragraph describes the moment that the tsunami struck?
  A. The first paragraph
  B. The second paragraph
  C. The third paragraph
  D. The fourth paragraph

PLACES

a body from the ruins of Pompeii

PREPARE TO READ
Discuss these questions.

1. The person in the picture died nearly 2,000 years ago. What killed this person?

2. What kinds of disasters can destroy an entire town?

WORD FOCUS
Match the words with their definitions.

A.

1. abandoned __	**a.** left behind
2. collapse __	**b.** a digging place
3. excavation __	**c.** in a fearful and excited way
4. flee __	**d.** escape
5. frantically __	**e.** fall down

B.

1. lava __	**a.** a vacation place
2. prosperous __	**b.** push out material quickly and messily
3. resort __	**c.** a mountain that sends out liquid rock and fire
4. spew __	**d.** wealthy; successful
5. volcano __	**e.** very hot, liquid rock

SCAN
A. Guess the answer. Circle *a* or *b*.

Vesuvius is the name of a

a. king.   *b.* volcano.

B. Scan the passage quickly to check your answer.

Pompeii

The ancient Roman town of Pompeii sat at the foot of the giant **volcano** Vesuvius in southern Italy. The town and the volcano had lived peacefully side by side for years.

5 Pompeii's citizens lived a good life. Their town was a **prosperous** port and a popular **resort**. Many wealthy Romans had their vacation homes there. The theaters, shops, and temples were filled with activity. All this

10 ended on August 24 in the year 79 A.D.

At about noon on August 24, a great cloud of ash and rocks **spewed** out of the top of Vesuvius, ascending 20 kilometers into the air. The ash and rocks began to rain down on the

15 unsuspecting citizens of Pompeii and other nearby towns. Soon, the roofs of Pompeii were covered with a layer of volcanic material that was close to three meters thick. Buildings started **collapsing** under the heavy weight. By

20 this time, people had already started **fleeing** the town. Grabbing what possessions they could and calling **frantically** to their loved ones to join them, they escaped to the countryside, as far from the town as they

25 could go. By evening, most of the residents had left Pompeii.

But Vesuvius hadn't finished yet. All night long, it continued to spew rock and ash high into the air. The next morning, steaming **lava**

30 poured out of the volcano and rolled down its sides toward Pompeii. The lava buried the town in a layer so deep that only the tops of the very tallest buildings could be seen. Later, some people returned to the town to try to

35 dig their possessions out of the hardened lava, but of course no one could live there any more. The buried town lay **abandoned** for hundreds of years.

In 1748, the long-forgotten town was

40 rediscovered. Since then, a number of **excavations** have been made uncovering a great deal of information about ancient Roman life. Architecture, art, and other examples of Roman culture were all perfectly preserved by

45 the lava. Excavators have also uncovered the bodies of about 2,000 Pompeii citizens who, unable to escape the rushing wave of lava, became <u>frozen</u> in it forever.

WHICH MEANING?
What does *frozen* mean in line 48?

1 (*adjective*) very cold
2 (*adjective*) not moving
3 (*adjective*) unfriendly

CHECK YOUR COMPREHENSION

Read the passage again and answer the questions. Circle your answers.

MAIN IDEA
1. What is this passage mainly about?
   - **A.** The ancient Roman Empire
   - **B.** The last days of Pompeii
   - **C.** The volcanoes of Rome
   - **D.** The excavation of an ancient town

DETAIL
2. At about what time of day did Vesuvius begin to erupt?
   - **A.** Early in the morning
   - **B.** 12:00 noon
   - **C.** Late in the afternoon
   - **D.** At night

3. What happened to the buildings of Pompeii?
   - **A.** They were mostly undamaged.
   - **B.** They were burned by fire from the volcano.
   - **C.** They were carried away by the flood of lava.
   - **D.** They fell down under the weight of rocks and ash.

4. What happened in 1748?
   - **A.** Pompeii was rediscovered.
   - **B.** Vesuvius erupted again.
   - **C.** A museum of Roman art was opened.
   - **D.** Pompeii's citizens returned to their homes.

INFERENCE
5. What is true about Pompeii?
   - **A.** Most of the citizens were poor.
   - **B.** It was a boring place to visit.
   - **C.** Very few people lived there.
   - **D.** It was on the coast.

TEXT ORGANIZATION
6. Which paragraph describes discoveries made by excavators in Pompeii?
   - **A.** The first paragraph
   - **B.** The second paragraph
   - **C.** The third paragraph
   - **D.** The fourth paragraph

THINGS

PREPARE TO READ
Discuss these questions.

1. This photo shows a disaster area in the city of Boston in 1919. What do you think caused it?

2. Molasses is sweet syrup, like honey. How can it be dangerous to people?

WORD FOCUS
Match the words with their definitions.

A.

1. bring about __   **a.** following
2. drown __   **b.** easy to see
3. ensuing __   **c.** quiet; difficult to hear
4. evident __   **d.** cause to happen
5. muffled __   **e.** die in water

B.

1. sticky __   **a.** destroy
2. storage __   **b.** throw
3. toss __   **c.** like glue or tape
4. warehouse __   **d.** keeping things
5. wreck __   **e.** a building for keeping things in

SCAN
A. Guess the answer. Circle *a* or *b*.

A Boston company built a storage tank that could hold _____ of liters of molasses.

a. thousands   *b.* millions

B. Scan the passage quickly to check your answer.

The Great Molasses Flood

Molasses, a sweet syrup made from sugarcane, is used in baking. There's an old saying "as slow as molasses in January" because cold molasses becomes very thick and doesn't pour
5 easily. This was proven to be an inaccurate description in January of 1919, when a giant wave of molasses rushed through the streets of Boston at a speed of almost 60 kilometers an hour. It caused a disaster that could have
10 been avoided. It was **brought about** by the stupidity of one man.

A Boston company built a huge molasses **storage** tank. The tank was over 16 meters tall and 30 meters wide. When it was finished,
15 no one tested the tank to see if it leaked. Millions of liters of the **sticky**, sweet liquid were added to the tank. It did leak. Rather than fix the leaks, the man in charge painted the tank brown, the color of molasses, so the
20 leaks were not so **evident**.

Just after noon on January 15, people in the area heard a loud cracking noise followed by a **muffled** roar. The leaking storage tank had exploded, sending a ten-meter-high wave of
25 molasses flowing through the nearby streets.

It **wrecked** everything in its path—people's homes, **warehouses**, even part of the local train line. It **tossed** wagons, horses, and furniture into the air. Several people and animals were
30 **drowned** by the swiftly moving wave of syrup. All in all, 21 people, 12 horses, and one cat were killed, and 150 people were injured.

The molasses was almost a meter deep in the streets around the storage tank. Rescue
35 work was nearly impossible because rescuers couldn't walk through the sticky <u>stuff</u>. It sucked the shoes right off their feet. Molasses filled the cellars of neighborhood houses, and it took months to pump it out. The streets
40 and buildings had to be washed with salt water because fresh water couldn't remove the stuff. As a result of the flood and **ensuing** clean up, Boston Harbor was dark brown for six months. To this day, some people claim
45 that on a hot day they can still smell molasses in the neighborhood.

WHICH MEANING?
What does *stuff* mean in line 36?

1 (*noun*) possessions
2 (*verb*) fill
3 (*noun*) substance

CHECK YOUR COMPREHENSION

Read the passage again and answer the questions. Circle your answers.

MAIN IDEA

1. What is this passage mainly about?

A. A disaster in Boston
B. Clean up of Boston Harbor
C. Different ways to use molasses
D. The history of a molasses company

DETAIL

2. Why did the man paint the storage tank brown?

A. Brown was his favorite color.
B. He had many extra liters of brown paint.
C. He didn't want to fix the leaks in the tank.
D. A paint company gave him free brown paint.

3. How fast did the wave of molasses move?

A. Ten meters an hour
B. Sixteen meters an hour
C. Sixteen kilometers an hour
D. Sixty kilometers an hour

4. What happened when the molasses rushed through the streets?

A. Boats sank in the harbor.
B. People left the area by train.
C. Animals and people were killed.
D. Horses ran through the molasses-filled streets.

INFERENCE

5. What was the "muffled roar"?

A. The angry shouts of neighborhood residents
B. The noise of a train stuck in the molasses
C. The screams of frightened people
D. The sound of rushing molasses

TEXT REFERENCE

6. In line 14, *When it was finished*, what does the word *it* refer to?

A. The molasses
B. The company
C. The paint
D. The tank

VOCABULARY REVIEW

WORD SEARCH

Find and circle the vocabulary below. Then look for a word in the first line of the puzzle to fill in the blank: The world will never forget the _____ of 2004.

abandon
collapse
ensuing
evident
excavation
frantically
lava
muffled
prosperous
wreck

T	S	U	N	T	A	E	M	I	M	U	Q	P	O	O
K	K	C	D	M	N	B	O	W	J	Q	R	H	X	P
C	K	W	F	S	C	E	B	C	D	T	X	J	J	G
E	I	G	U	L	N	F	D	R	C	R	U	P	O	U
Z	M	I	P	T	S	O	B	I	Z	G	K	S	Z	Y
N	N	K	P	R	F	E	I	V	V	R	C	B	X	S
G	W	G	L	C	O	M	S	T	V	E	E	F	F	D
Y	N	T	F	V	U	S	Q	P	A	D	R	F	S	T
A	A	D	H	F	D	Y	P	P	A	V	W	E	W	P
M	Z	B	F	B	L	Y	L	E	I	L	A	K	Q	Z
Y	L	L	A	C	I	T	N	A	R	F	L	C	K	O
E	E	O	F	N	X	Y	Z	E	V	O	O	O	X	V
D	F	C	F	O	D	X	M	W	L	A	U	W	C	E
F	I	W	M	R	C	O	K	M	K	G	F	S	S	W
M	S	P	I	D	Y	N	N	U	F	Q	Z	D	D	I

WORDS IN CONTEXT

Fill in the blanks with words from each box.

drifted	disaster	inland	leak	reason

1. When there is hot weather _____, it's often cooler by the sea.

2. The storm destroyed many people's homes. It was a terrible _____.

3. The leaves fell into the water and _____ down the stream.

4. The sky was blue, so we had no _____ to expect the storm.

5. Rain always gets into our house because there's a _____ in the roof.

frozen	spewed	brought about	storage	tossed

6. It wasn't just good luck. Your success was _____ by your hard work.

7. This house has small closets. We need more _____ space.

8. When the children saw the huge dog, they were _____ with fear.

9. He _____ the ball in the wrong direction, and it hit the window.

10. The volcano _____ lava all night long.

| frantically | prosperous | stuff | wrecked | abandoned |

11. The wind last night blew down several old trees and _____ several houses.

12. Everybody _____ the beach because a big storm was approaching.

13. This is a very _____ town where almost everyone has a good job.

14. We put a lot of _____ into storage.

15. We arrived at the station late and ran _____ to catch the train.

WORD FAMILIES

Fill in the blanks with words from each box.

| **avoidance** (*noun*) | **avoid** (*verb*) | **avoidable** (*adjective*) |

1. Most problems are _____ if you plan carefully.

2. Everyone should _____ driving today because it's snowing hard.

| **stickiness** (*noun*) | **stick** (*verb*) | **sticky** (*adjective*) |

3. You can _____ those photos to the page with glue.

4. The child's hands and face were very _____ after eating bread with jelly.

| **evidence** (*noun*) | **evident** (*adjective*) | **evidently** (*adverb*) |

5. Takeshi talks about Atsuko all the time. His love for her is _____.

6. I know the cat ate my sandwich. The teeth marks on the bread are _____ of that.

WRONG WORD

One word in each group does not fit. Circle the word.

1. raft	car	ship	boat
2. hill	volcano	mountain	river
3. colleague	boss	cousin	employee
4. garbage	debris	trash	possessions
5. ice	rocks	lava	ash
6. rich	poor	wealthy	prosperous
7. flee	stay	run	escape

TRUE OR FALSE?

Are the following sentences true or false? Circle your answers.

1. A warehouse is a place to live.   TRUE   FALSE
2. It's very cold inside a volcano.   TRUE   FALSE
3. If you can't swim, you could drown.   TRUE   FALSE
4. A resort is a place to study.   TRUE   FALSE
5. A turtle runs more swiftly than a rabbit.   TRUE   FALSE
6. A tsunami is caused by an earthquake.   TRUE   FALSE
7. Molasses is sticky stuff.   TRUE   FALSE

WHAT ABOUT YOU?

Speaking

Ask your partner these questions.

1. What can you do swiftly?

2. What household jobs do you try to avoid?

3. What would you like to do at a resort?

4. Do you prefer disaster movies or horror movies?

5. Would you prefer to live inland or near the sea? Why?

Writing

Now write about your partner. Use your partner's answers to the questions.

Example: <u>Mika can read swiftly</u>.

1. _____

2. _____

3. _____

4. _____

5. _____

READING QUIZ

Read the passage and answer the questions. Circle your answers.

Weeks of rain combined with the melting snow of spring brought about a small disaster in Springfield last weekend. The Black River had been rising all week.
5 Around 6:00 last Friday evening, residents were cautioned by authorities that the river could rise high enough to flood the downtown area. Because of this warning, most Springfield residents
10 were able to flee the area before the flood occurred.

Around midnight, a muffled sound was heard as water from the river rushed swiftly through the streets of
15 Springfield's shopping district. The water rose to half a meter in some places.

An abandoned warehouse near the train station collapsed from the force of the rushing water. A water storage tank
20 was also wrecked by the flood. Fortunately, no other major damage was reported. Early Saturday morning, several groups of children were seen floating rafts down the water-filled streets. By late afternoon,
25 however, the water level had dropped to a few centimeters, and by Sunday morning it was gone.

Stores in downtown Springfield will remain closed today and tomorrow.
30 Curious people are asked to stay away from the area until it has been cleaned up. The streets are filled with debris which could cause accidents.

MAIN IDEA

1. What is a good headline for this article?
   A. Flood Clean-up
   B. Warehouse Collapses
   C. Disaster in Springfield
   D. Rafting on the Black River

DETAIL

2. What happened at 6:00 on Friday evening?
   A. The river flooded downtown Springfield.
   B. Springfield residents got a warning.
   C. A storage tank was wrecked.
   D. Children played on rafts.

INFERENCE

3. Why are people asked to stay away from the downtown area?
   A. The stores are closed.
   B. The streets are dangerous.
   C. The flood water is cold.
   D. An accident occurred there.

TEXT ORGANIZATION

4. Which paragraph describes damage caused by the flood?
   A. The first paragraph
   B. The second paragraph
   C. The third paragraph
   D. The fourth paragraph

VOCABULARY

5. What does *muffled* in line 12 mean?
   A. Loud
   B. Scary
   C. Ugly
   D. Quiet

6. What does *debris* in line 32 mean?
   A. Trash
   B. Water
   C. Cars
   D. Ice

VOCABULARY SELF-QUIZ

You can use these word lists to quiz yourself.
1. First, write your translations next to the English words. Study them for a while.
2. Then, quiz yourself. Cover up the English words. You should only look at your translations.
3. Try to remember the English words and write them down. How many words can you remember?

Unit 1 DATING

PEOPLE	TRANSLATION	TEST YOURSELF
average		
celebrity		
client		
complaint		
consultation		
fee		
insist		
luxurious		
match		
potential		

PLACES		
aisle		
chat		
embellish		
environment		
inspire		
intention		
location		
phenomenon		
pick out		
skeptical		

THINGS		
approximately		
back out		
eldest		
ensure		
instinct		
judgment		
show up		
suitable		
trust		
unlikely		

Unit 2 DOLPHINS

PEOPLE	TRANSLATION	TEST YOURSELF
adapt		
captivity		
habitat		
ironically		
pen		
priority		
process		
rehabilitate		
stress		
tide		

PLACES		
biologist		
euthanize		
gear		
lethal		
mission		
presumably		
severe		
staff		
stranded		
surgery		

THINGS		
blush		
disrupt		
extinction		
image		
maturity		
mere		
navigate		
reproduction		
snoop		
theory		

Unit 3 SOCCER

PEOPLE	TRANSLATION	TEST YOURSELF
convince		
distinct		
faze		
heighten		
media		
outshine		
penalty		
spokesperson		
trend		
wild		

PLACES		
debate		
establish		
govern		
obsessed		
outlaw		
remotely		
soldier		
spectator		
trip		
trophy		

THINGS		
break into		
conduct		
display		
hold on to		
inanimate		
ransom		
replica		
sculptor		
victory		
whirlwind		

Unit 4 BEAUTY

PEOPLE	TRANSLATION	TEST YOURSELF
cosmetic		
everlasting		
fantasy		
glamorous		
inheritance		
principle		
quest		
sag		
tattoo		
transformation		

PLACES		
bearable		
elect		
financial		
genuine		
grade		
pressure		
prized		
self-proclaimed		
standard		
virtue		

THINGS		
appropriate		
dye		
essential		
feminine		
guarantee		
marketing		
masculine		
promote		
reluctant		
target		

Unit 5 FANTASY

PEOPLE	TRANSLATION	TEST YOURSELF
aluminum		
ascend		
authorities		
fine		
helium		
parachute		
regulations		
shiver		
tangle		
violate		

PLACES

explore		
fulfill		
harmony		
offering		
paradise		
precious		
region		
starvation		
unique		
utopia		

THINGS

aristocrat		
astronaut		
ball		
bold		
elegant		
escort		
finery		
racetrack		
royal		
zoom		

Unit 6 REPTILES

PEOPLE	TRANSLATION	TEST YOURSELF
blame		
carry on		
cobra		
donate		
feat		
lifespan		
major		
perish		
pursue		
retire		

PLACES		
bacteria		
cautious		
claw		
consume		
dart		
forked		
keep away		
lizard		
plod		
unsuspecting		

THINGS		
amphibians		
creep		
mine		
peer		
scaly		
scan		
slimy		
slithery		
swamp		
thorn		

Unit 7 FORTUNE-TELLING

PEOPLE	TRANSLATION	TEST YOURSELF
accurately		
assassination		
astrology		
charity		
earthquake		
palm		
predict		
stray		
vegetarian		
vision		

PLACES		
architecture		
container		
guidance		
incense		
interpret		
intricate		
noted		
pray		
stream		
temple		

THINGS		
brew		
discard		
drain		
fragrant		
handle		
ladder		
liquid		
saucer		
steaming		
unexpectedly		

Unit 8 DISASTERS

PEOPLE	TRANSLATION	TEST YOURSELF
avoid		
colleague		
debris		
disaster		
drift		
inland		
leak		
raft		
swiftly		
tsunami		

PLACES		
abandoned		
collapse		
excavation		
flee		
frantically		
lava		
prosperous		
resort		
spew		
volcano		

THINGS		
bring about		
drown		
ensuing		
evident		
muffled		
sticky		
storage		
toss		
warehouse		
wreck		

VOCABULARY INDEX

The number refers to the page where the word appears in the reading passages.

L

ladder **67**
lava **75**
leak **73**, 77
lethal **15**, 21, 53, 55
lifespan **53**, 61
liquid **67**, 71, 77
lizard **55**, 57, 61
location **5**, 11, 61
luxurious **3**, 51

M

major **53**, 61, 63, 81
marketing **37**, 41
masculine **37**, 41
match **3**, 5, 7, 11
maturity **17**, 21
media **23**
mere **17**, 21
mine **57**
mission **15**, 21, 33
muffled **77**, 81

N

navigate **17**, 21
noted **65**

O

obsessed **25**, 31, 33, 71
offering **45**, 65
outlaw **25**
outshine **23**

P

palm **63**, 65, 71
parachute **43**
paradise **45**
peer **57**, 61, 63
pen **13**, 15, 21, 53
penalty **23**, 25, 31
perish **53**, 55, 61
phenomenon **5**, 15
pick out **5**, 11
plod **55**, 57
potential **3**, 5
pray **65**, 71
precious **45**, 57
predict **63**, 65, 67, 71
pressure **35**, 37, 41, 51
presumably **15**, 21

principle 33
priority **13**, 15, 21
prized **35**
process **13**
promote **37**, 41
prosperous **75**
pursue **53**
  (pursuit **55**, 57)

Q

quest **33**, 41, 45, 57

R

racetrack **47**
raft **73**, 81
ransom **27**
region **45**, 51, 55
regulations **43**
rehabilitate **13**, 15, 21
reluctant **37**, 41
remotely **25**, 31, 45, 57
replica **27**
reproduction **17**, 21
resort **75**
retire **53**
royal **47**, 51

S

sag **33**
saucer **67**
scaly **57**
scan **57**
sculptor **27**
self-proclaimed **35**
severe **15**, 21
shiver **43**
show up **7**, 11, 25
skeptical **5**, 11
slimy **57**
slithery **57**
snoop **17**, 27
soldier **25**
spectator **25**, 31
spew **75**
spokesperson **23**, 35, 37
staff **15**, 21
standard **35**, 41
starvation **45**, 73
steaming **67**, 75
sticky **77**
storage **77**, 81

stranded **15**, 21
stray **63**, 73
stream **65**
stress **13**, 17, 21
suitable **7**, 11, 61
surgery **15**, 21, 33
swamp **57**
swiftly **73**, 77, 81

T

tangle **43**
target **37**
tattoo **33**, 41
temple **65**, 75
theory **17**
thorn **57**
tide **13**, 21
toss **77**
transformation **33**, 41
trend **23**, 31, 37
trip **25**, 31
trophy **25**, 27, 31
trust **7**, 11, 13
tsunami **73**

U

unexpectedly **67**, 73
unique **45**, 51, 63
unlikely **7**, 15
unsuspecting **55**, 61, 75
utopia **45**

V

vegetarian **63**
victory **27**, 31
violate **43**
virtue **35**, 41
vision **63**, 71
volcano **75**

W

warehouse **77**, 81
whirlwind **27**
wild **23**, 31, 57
wreck **77**, 81

Z

zoom **47**

COMMON IRREGULAR VERBS

INFINITIVE	SIMPLE PAST	PAST PARTICIPLE
be	was/were	been
become	became	become
begin	began	begun
bite	bit	bitten
break	broke	broken
bring	brought	brought
build	built	built
burn	burned/burnt	burned/burnt
buy	bought	bought
catch	caught	caught
choose	chose	chosen
come	came	come
cost	cost	cost
creep	crept	crept
cut	cut	cut
dig	dug	dug
do	did	done
dream	dreamed/dreamt	dreamed/dreamt
drink	drank	drunk
drive	drove	driven
eat	ate	eaten
fall	fell	fallen
feed	fed	fed
feel	felt	felt
fight	fought	fought
find	found	found
fit	fit/fitted	fit/fitted
flee	fled	fled
fly	flew	flown
freeze	froze	frozen
get	got	gotten
give	gave	given
go/goes	went	gone
grow	grew	grown
hang	hung	hung
have/has	had	had
hear	heard	heard
hide	hid	hidden
hit	hit	hit
hold	held	held
hurt	hurt	hurt
keep	kept	kept
know	knew	known
lead	led	led

INFINITIVE	SIMPLE PAST	PAST PARTICIPLE
leave	left	left
lend	lent	lent
let	let	let
lose	lost	lost
make	made	made
mean	meant	meant
meet	met	met
pay	paid	paid
prove	proved	proved/proven
put	put	put
read	read	read
ride	rode	ridden
rise	rose	risen
run	ran	run
say	said	said
see	saw	seen
seek	sought	sought
sell	sold	sold
set	set	set
shake	shook	shaken
shave	shaved	shaved/shaven
shoot	shot	shot
show	showed	showed/shown
sit	sat	sat
sleep	slept	slept
speak	spoke	spoken
speed	sped	sped
spend	spent	spent
stand	stood	stood
steal	stole	stolen
strike	struck	struck/stricken
swim	swam	swum
swing	swung	swung
take	took	taken
teach	taught	taught
tear	tore	torn
tell	told	told
think	thought	thought
throw	threw	thrown
understand	understood	understood
wear	wore	worn
win	win	win
write	wrote	written